The Responsibility of Intellectuals

ALSO BY NOAM CHOMSKY

The
Responsibility
of
Intellectuals

Noam Chomsky

THE NEW PRESS

25 YEARS

NEW YORK
LONDON

© 2017 by The New Press
Preface © 2017 by L. Valeria Galvao-Wasserman-Chomsky
All rights reserved.
No part of this book may be reproduced, in any form, without written permission from the publisher.

Page 143 constitutes an extension of this copyright page.

Requests for permission to reproduce selections from this book should be mailed to: Permissions Department, The New Press, 120 Wall Street, 31st floor, New York, NY 10005.

Published in the United States by The New Press, New York, 2017
Distributed by Perseus Distribution

ISBN 978-1-62097-343-1 (hc)
ISBN 978-1-62097-364-6 (e-book)
CIP data is available

The New Press publishes books that promote and enrich public discussion and understanding of the issues vital to our democracy and to a more equitable world. These books are made possible by the enthusiasm of our readers; the support of a committed group of donors, large and small; the collaboration of our many partners in the independent media and the not-for-profit sector; booksellers, who often hand-sell New Press books; librarians; and above all by our authors.

www.thenewpress.com

Book design and composition by Lovedog Studio
This book was set in Sabon

Printed in the United States of America

10 9 8 7 6 5 4 3 2

Contents

The Responsibility of Intellectuals

Preface

The concept of "intellectuals" is a rather curious one. Who qualifies?

The question arises in an instructive way in Dwight Macdonald's classic 1945 essay "The Responsibility of Intellectuals." The essay is a bitter and sardonic critique of distinguished thinkers pontificating about the "collective guilt" of German refugees who were barely surviving in the ruins of wartime disaster. He contrasts their self-righteous contempt for the miserable survivors with the reaction of soldiers of the victorious army, who recognize the humanity of the victims and sympathize with their plight. The former are intellectuals, the latter not.

Macdonald ends his essay with simple words: "It is a great thing to be able to see what is right under your nose."

What of the responsibility of intellectuals? Those who qualify for the title have a degree of privilege conferred by this status, yielding opportunity beyond the norm. Opportunity confers responsibility—which, in turn, poses choices, sometimes hard ones.

One choice is to follow the path of integrity, wherever it may lead. Another is to put such concerns aside, passively adopting the conventions instituted by structures of authority. The task in the latter case, then, is to carry out faithfully the instructions of those who hold the reins of power, to be loyal and faithful servants, not after reflective judgment but by reflexive conformism. That is a fine way to evade the moral and intellectual difficulties of challenge and to escape what can be painful consequences of seeking to bend the moral arc of the universe towards justice.

The alternatives are familiar. Thus we distinguish the commissars and apparatchiks from the dissidents who confront the challenge and face the consequences—which vary, depending on the nature of the society. Many dissidents are well-known and rightly honored, and their harsh treatment is rightly denounced with fervor and outrage: Václav Havel, Ai Weiwei, Shirin Ebadi, and a distinguished list of others. We also rightly condemn the apologists for the evil society, who offer at most tepid criticism of "mistakes" of rulers who they routinely describe as benign in intent.

Others are missing from the list of honored dissidents, for example, the six leading Latin American intellectuals, Jesuit priests, who were brutally murdered by Salvadoran forces fresh from renewed training by U.S. forces, acting on the specific orders of the U.S. client government. In fact, they are scarcely known at all. Few even know their names, or recall the events. The official orders to murder them have yet to appear in the United States anywhere near the mainstream, not because they are secret: they were published prominently in the mainstream Spanish press.

This is not an exception. It is the rule. The facts are not in the least obscure. They are well-known to activists who protested the horrendous U.S. crimes in Central America, and to scholarship. In the *Cambridge History of the Cold War*, John Coatsworth writes that from 1960 to "the

Soviet collapse in 1990, the numbers of political prisoners, torture victims, and executions of non-violent political dissenters in Latin America vastly exceeded those in the Soviet Union and its East European satellites."

When we turn to coverage in media and intellectual journals, we find that the picture is reversed. To take one of many striking illustrations, Edward Herman and I compared the *New York Times* coverage of the murder of a Polish priest—whose assassins were quickly found and punished—with the murder of one hundred religious martyrs in El Salvador, including Archbishop Óscar Romero and four American churchwomen, whose assassins were long concealed, while the crimes were denied by U.S. officials and the victims subjected to official contempt. The coverage of the murdered priest in an enemy state vastly exceeded that of one hundred religious martyrs in the U.S. client state, and was radically different in style in the way predicted by a propaganda model of the media.[1] This is only one illustration of a highly consistent pattern over many years.

One choice
is to follow
the path
of integrity,
wherever it
may lead.

To be sure, there might be some explanation other than service to power. Occasionally—very rarely—the facts receive some notice, accompanied by an effort to explain them away. In the case of the religious martyrs, an alternative explanation was offered in a derisive response by the distinguished U.S. journalist Nicholas Lemann, national correspondent of the liberal *Atlantic Monthly*: "the discrepancy can be explained by saying the press tends to focus on only a few things at a time," Lemann writes, and "the U.S. press was most focused on Poland."

Lemann's explanation is easily tested by a look at the *New York Times* index, which shows that in the relevant period coverage of the two countries was virtually identical, a little higher for El Salvador. But in an intellectual environment of "alternative facts," details like this hardly matter.[2]

In practice, the honorific term "dissident" is reserved in practice for dissidents in enemy states. The six murdered Latin American intellectuals, the archbishop, and the many others like them in U.S. client states who protest state crimes and are therefore murdered, tortured, or imprisoned are not termed "dissidents" (if they are mentioned at all).

Terminology at home differs as well. There were, for example, intellectuals who protested the Vietnam War, for varying reasons. To take prominent examples who illustrate the bounds of the elite spectrum, journalist Joseph Alsop protested that the U.S. intervention was too limited, while Arthur Schlesinger retorted that escalation probably wouldn't succeed and would prove to be too costly for ourselves. Nevertheless, he added, "we all pray" that Alsop will be right in thinking that U.S. force may prevail, and if it does, "we may all be saluting the wisdom and statesmanship of the American government" in winning victory while leaving "the tragic country gutted and devastated by bombs, burned by napalm, turned into a wasteland by chemical defoliation, a land of ruin and wreck," with its "political and institutional fabric" pulverized.

Alsop and Schlesinger are not termed "dissidents." Rather, they are, respectively, a hawk and a dove, at the opposite ends of the spectrum of legitimate criticism of the U.S. war.

There are, to be sure, some who are off the spectrum entirely, but they are not "dissidents" either. As Kennedy-Johnson National Security Adviser McGeorge Bundy explained in the establishment journal *Foreign Affairs*, they are "wild men in the wings," who raise objections of principle to U.S. aggression, not merely tactical questions about feasibility and cost.

Bundy was writing in 1967, at the time when the bitterly anti-Communist military historian and Vietnam specialist Bernard Fall, highly respected in the U.S. government and mainstream opinion, feared that "Vietnam as a cultural and historic entity . . . is threatened with extinction . . . [as] . . . the countryside literally dies under the blows of the largest military machine ever unleashed on an area of this size." But it was only "wild men in the wings" who questioned the justice of the American cause.

As the war ended in 1975, intellectuals across the mainstream spectrum provided their interpretations of what had happened. They ranged across the Alsop-Schlesinger spectrum. At the extreme dovish end, Anthony Lewis wrote that the intervention began with "blundering efforts to do good" ("blundering" because it failed, "efforts to do good" by doctrinal principle, evidence unnecessary), but by 1969 it was clear that the intervention was a mistake because the United States "could not impose a solution except at a price too costly to itself."

At the same time polls showed that about 70 percent of the population regarded the war as not "a mistake" but "fundamentally wrong and immoral." Like the soldiers of 1945 who could appreciate the plight of miserable German refugees, they are not intellectuals.

The examples are typical. Opposition to the war peaked in 1970, after the Nixon-Kissinger invasion of Cambodia. Right at that time, political scientist Charles Kadushin conducted an extensive study of attitudes of "elite intellectuals." On Vietnam, he found that overwhelmingly, they adopted a "pragmatic" stance, criticizing the war as a mistake that proved too costly. "Wild men in the wings" were barely at the level of statistical error.[3]

Washington's wars in Indochina were the worst crime of the post–World War II era. The worst crime of this millennium is the U.S.-U.K. invasion of Iraq, with horrifying consequences throughout the region and no end in sight. The intellectual elite rose to the occasion in the familiar way. Barack Obama was highly praised by liberal intellectuals for adopting the stance of the doves. In Obama's own words, "Over the past decade, American troops have made extraordinary sacrifices to give Iraqis an opportunity to claim their own future" but "The hard truth is we have not seen the end of American sacrifice in Iraq." The war was a "grave mistake," a "strategic blunder," far too costly to us[4]—a judgment that may be compared to that of many Russian generals about the Soviet decision to intervene in Afghanistan.

The pattern generalizes. There should hardly be any need to review examples—as has been done extensively in print, with no detectable effect on elite intellectual doctrine.

There are no dissidents within our shores, nor commissars and apparatchiks. Only wild men in the wings and responsible intellectuals, who qualify as true experts. The responsibility of the experts is spelled out by one of the most foremost and distinguished of them. One qualifies as an "expert," Henry Kissinger explains, by "elaborating and defining" the consensus of one's constituency "at a high level"—the "constituency" being those who establish the framework within which experts execute the assigned tasks.

The categories are quite conventional, going back to the earliest usage of the concept "intellectual" in the contemporary sense during the Dreyfus affair in France. The leading figure of the Dreyfusards, Émile Zola, was sentenced to a year in prison for the infamy of calling for justice for the falsely accused Alfred Dreyfus, and fled to England to escape further punishment. He was bitterly denounced by the "immortals" of the French Academy. The Dreyfusards were true "wild men in the wings." They were guilty of "one of the most ridiculous eccentricities of our time," in the words of Academician Ferdinand Brunetière: "the pretension of raising writers, scientists, professors and philologists to the rank of supermen," who dare to "treat our generals as idiots, our social institutions as absurd and our traditions as unhealthy." They dared to interfere with matters properly left to "experts"—to "responsible men," "technocratic and policy-oriented intellectuals," in the contemporary terminology of liberal discourse.

So what then is the responsibility of intellectuals? They always have a choice. In enemy states, they can choose to be commissars or dissidents. In U.S. client states, in the modern period, the choice can be bitter beyond words. At home, they can choose to be responsible experts or wild men in the wings.

And then there is always the choice of following Macdonald's good advice: "It is a great thing to be able to see what is right under your nose"—and to have the simple honesty to tell it as it is.

Part I

The Responsibility of Intellectuals

Twenty years ago, Dwight Macdonald published a series of articles in *Politics* on the responsibility of peoples and, specifically, the responsibility of intellectuals. I read them as an undergraduate, in the years just after the war, and had occasion to read them again a few months ago. They seem to me to have lost none of their power or persuasiveness. Macdonald is concerned with the question of war guilt. He asks the question: To what extent were the German or Japanese people responsible for the atrocities committed by their governments? And, quite properly, he turns the question back to us: To what extent are the British or American people responsible for the vicious terror bombings of civilians, perfected as a technique of warfare by the Western democracies and reaching their culmination in Hiroshima and Nagasaki, surely among the most unspeakable crimes in history. To an undergraduate in 1945–46—to anyone whose political and moral consciousness had been formed by the horrors of the 1930s, by the war in Ethiopia, the Russian purge, the "China Incident," the Spanish Civil War, the Nazi atrocities, the Western reaction to these events and, in part, complicity in them—these questions had particular significance and poignancy.

With respect to the responsibility of intellectuals, there are still other, equally disturbing questions. Intellectuals are in a position to expose the lies of governments, to analyze actions according to their causes and motives and often hidden intentions. In the Western world, at least, they have the power that comes from political liberty, from access to information and freedom of expression. For a privileged minority, Western democracy provides the leisure, the facilities, and the training to seek the truth lying hidden behind the veil of distortion and misrepresentation, ideology and class interest, through which the events of current history are presented to us. The responsibilities of intellectuals, then, are much deeper than what

Macdonald calls the "responsibility of people," given the unique privileges that intellectuals enjoy.

The issues that Macdonald raised are as pertinent today as they were twenty years ago. We can hardly avoid asking ourselves to what extent the American people bear responsibility for the savage American assault on a largely helpless rural population in Vietnam, still another atrocity in what Asians see as the "Vasco da Gama era" of world history. As for those of us who stood by in silence and apathy as this catastrophe slowly took shape over the past dozen years—on what page of history do we find our proper place? Only the most insensible can escape these questions. I want to return to them, later on, after a few scattered remarks about the responsibility of intellectuals and how, in practice, they go about meeting this responsibility in the mid-1960s.

+ + + +

IT IS THE RESPONSIBILITY of intellectuals to speak the truth and to expose lies. This, at least, may seem enough of a truism to pass over without comment. Not so, however. For the modern

Intellectuals are
in a position to
expose the lies
of governments,
to analyze actions
according to their
causes and motives
and often
hidden intentions.

intellectual, it is not at all obvious. Thus we have Martin Heidegger writing, in a pro-Hitler declaration of 1933, that "truth is the revelation of that which makes a people certain, clear, and strong in its action and knowledge"; it is only this kind of "truth" that one has a responsibility to speak. Americans tend to be more forthright. When Arthur Schlesinger was asked by the *New York Times* in November 1965 to explain the contradiction between his published account of the Bay of Pigs incident and the story he had given the press at the time of the attack, he simply remarked that he had lied; and a few days later, he went on to compliment the *Times* for also having suppressed information on the planned invasion, in "the national interest," as this term was defined by the group of arrogant and deluded men of whom Schlesinger gives such a flattering portrait in his recent account of the Kennedy administration. It is of no particular interest that one man is quite happy to lie in behalf of a cause which he knows to be unjust; but it is significant that such events provoke so little response in the intellectual community—for example, no one has said that there is something strange in the offer of a major chair in the humanities to a historian who feels it to be his duty to persuade the world that an American-sponsored invasion of a nearby country is nothing of the sort. And what of the incredible sequence of lies on the part of our government and its spokesmen concerning such matters as negotiations in Vietnam? The facts are known to all who care to know. The press, foreign and domestic, has presented documentation to refute each falsehood as it appears. But the power of the government's propaganda apparatus is such that the citizen who does not undertake a research project on the subject can hardly hope to confront government pronouncements with fact.[1]

The deceit and distortion surrounding the American invasion of Vietnam is by now so familiar that it has lost its power to shock. It is therefore useful to recall that although new levels of cynicism are constantly being reached, their clear antecedents were accepted at home with quiet toleration. It is a useful exercise to compare government statements at the time of the invasion of Guatemala in 1954 with Eisenhower's admission—to be more accurate, his boast—a decade later that American planes were sent "to help the invaders" (*New York Times*, October 14, 1965). Nor is it only in moments of crisis that duplicity is considered perfectly in order. "New Frontiersmen," for example, have scarcely distinguished themselves by a passionate concern for historical accuracy, even when they are not being called upon to provide a "propaganda cover" for ongoing actions. For example, Arthur Schlesinger (*New York Times*, February 6, 1966) describes the bombing of North Vietnam and the massive escalation of military commitment in early 1965 as based on a "perfectly rational argument": "So long as the Vietcong thought they were going to win the war, they obviously would not be interested in any kind of negotiated settlement."

The date is important. Had this statement been made six months earlier, one could attribute it to ignorance. But this statement appeared after the UN, North Vietnamese, and Soviet initiatives had been front-page news for months. It was already public knowledge that these initiatives had preceded the escalation of February 1965 and, in fact, continued for several weeks after the bombing began. Correspondents in Washington tried desperately to find some explanation for the startling deception that had been revealed. Chalmers Roberts, for example, wrote in the *Boston Globe* on November 19 with unconscious irony:

> *[Late February 1965] hardly seemed to Washington to be a propitious moment for negotiations [since] Mr. Johnson . . . had just ordered the first bombing of North Vietnam in an effort to bring Hanoi to a conference table where the bargaining chips on both sides would be more closely matched.*

Coming at that moment, Schlesinger's statement is less an example of deceit than of contempt—contempt for an audience that can be expected to tolerate such behavior with silence, if not approval.[2]

+ + + +

TO TURN TO SOMEONE closer to the actual formation and implementation of policy, consider

SPECIOUS

some of the reflections of Walt Rostow, a man who, according to Schlesinger, brought a "spacious historical view" to the conduct of foreign affairs in the Kennedy administration.[3] According to his analysis, the guerrilla warfare in Indo-China in 1946 was launched by Stalin,[4] and Hanoi initiated the guerrilla war against South Vietnam in 1958 (*View from the Seventh Floor*, pp. 39 and 152). Similarly, the Communist planners probed the "free world spectrum of defense" in northern Azerbaijan and Greece (where Stalin "supported substantial guerrilla warfare"—*ibid*., pp. 36 and 148), operating from plans carefully laid in 1945. And in Central Europe, the Soviet Union was not "prepared to accept a solution which would remove the dangerous tensions from Central Europe at the risk of even slowly staged corrosion of Communism in East Germany" (*ibid*., p. 156).

It is interesting to compare these observations with studies by scholars actually concerned with historical events. The remark about Stalin's initiating the first Vietnamese war in 1946 does not even merit refutation. As to Hanoi's purported initiative of 1958, the situation is more clouded. But even government sources[5] concede that in 1959 Hanoi received the first direct reports of what Diem[6] referred to as his own Algerian war and that only after this did they lay their plans to involve themselves in this struggle. In fact, in December 1958, Hanoi made another of its many attempts—rebuffed once again by Saigon and the United States—to establish diplomatic and commercial relations with the Saigon government on the basis of the status quo.[7] Rostow offers no evidence of Stalin's support for the Greek guerrillas; in fact, though the historical record is far from clear, it seems that Stalin was by no means pleased with the adventurism of the Greek guerrillas, who, from his point of view, were upsetting the satisfactory postwar imperialist settlement.[8]

Rostow's remarks about Germany are more interesting still. He does not see fit to mention, for example, the Russian notes of March–April 1952, which proposed unification of Germany under internationally supervised elections, with withdrawal of all troops within a year, *if* there was a guarantee that a reunified Germany would not

In addition to
this growing lack
of concern
for truth,
we find a real or
feigned naiveté
about American
actions that
reaches startling
proportions.

be permitted to join a Western military alliance.[9] And he has also momentarily forgotten his own characterization of the strategy of the Truman and Eisenhower administrations: "to avoid any serious negotiation with the Soviet Union until the West could confront Moscow with German rearmament within an organized European framework, as a *fait accompli*"[10]—to be sure, in defiance of the Potsdam agreements.

But most interesting of all is Rostow's reference to Iran. The facts are that there was a Russian attempt to impose by force a pro-Soviet government in northern Azerbaijan that would grant the Soviet Union access to Iranian oil. This was rebuffed by superior Anglo-American force in 1946, at which point the more powerful imperialism obtained full rights to Iranian oil for itself, with the installation of a pro-Western government. We recall what happened when, for a brief period in the early 1950s, the only Iranian government with something of a popular base experimented with the curious idea that Iranian oil should belong to the Iranians. What is interesting, however, is the description of northern Azerbaijan as part of the "free world spectrum of defense." It is pointless, by now, to comment on the debasement of the phrase "free world." But by what law of nature does Iran, with its resources, fall within Western dominion? The bland assumption that it does is most revealing of deep-seated attitudes towards the conduct of foreign affairs.

+ + + +

IN ADDITION TO THIS growing lack of concern for truth, we find, in recent published statements, a real or feigned naiveté about American actions that reaches startling proportions. For example, Arthur Schlesinger, according to the *Times*, February 6, 1966, characterized our Vietnamese policies of 1954 as "part of our general program of international goodwill." Unless intended as irony, this remark shows either a colossal cynicism or the inability, on a scale that defies measurement, to comprehend elementary phenomena of contemporary history. Similarly, what is one to make of the testimony of Thomas Schelling before the House Foreign Affairs Committee, January 27, 1965, in which he discusses two great dangers if all Asia "goes Communist"?[11] First, this would exclude "the United States and what we call Western civilization from a large part of the world that is poor and colored and potentially hostile." Second, "a country like the United States probably cannot maintain self-confidence if just about the greatest thing it ever attempted, namely to create the basis for decency and prosperity and democratic government in the underdeveloped world, had to be acknowledged as a failure or as an attempt that we wouldn't try again." It surpasses belief that a person with even a minimal acquaintance with the record of American foreign policy could produce such statements.

It surpasses belief, that is, unless we look at the matter from a more historical point of view and place such statements in the context of the hypocritical moralism of the past; for example, of Woodrow Wilson, who was going to teach the Latin Americans the art of good government, and who wrote (1902) that it is "our peculiar duty" to teach colonial peoples "order and self-control [and] . . . the drill and habit of law and obedience." Or of the missionaries of the 1840s, who described the hideous and degrading opium wars as "the result of a great design of Providence to make the wickedness of men subserve his purposes of mercy toward China, in breaking through her wall of exclusion, and bringing the empire into more immediate contact with western and Christian nations." Or, to approach the present, of A.A. Berle, who, in commenting on the Dominican intervention, has the impertinence to attribute the problems of the Caribbean countries to imperialism—*Russian* imperialism.[12]

+ + + +

AS A FINAL EXAMPLE of this failure of skepticism, consider the remarks of Henry Kissinger in his concluding remarks at the Harvard-Oxford television debate on America's Vietnam policies. He observed, rather sadly, that what disturbs him most is that others question not our judgment, but our motives—a remarkable comment by a man whose professional concern is political analysis, that is, analysis of the actions of governments in terms of motives that are unexpressed in official propaganda and

It is an article
of faith that
American motives
are pure and
not subject
to analysis.

perhaps only dimly perceived by those whose acts they govern. No one would be disturbed by an analysis of the political behavior of the Russians, French, or Tanzanians questioning their motives and interpreting their actions by the long-range interests concealed behind their official rhetoric. But it is an article of faith that American motives are pure and not subject to analysis (see note 1). Although it is nothing new in American intellectual history—or, for that matter, in the general history of imperialist apologia—this innocence becomes increasingly distasteful as the power it serves grows more dominant in world affairs, and more capable, therefore, of the unconstrained viciousness that the mass media present to us each day. We are hardly the first power in history to combine material interests, great technological capacity, and an utter disregard for the suffering and misery of the lower orders. The long tradition of naiveté and self-righteousness that disfigures our intellectual history, however, must serve as a warning to the third world, if such a warning is needed, as to how our protestations of sincerity and benign intent are to be interpreted.

The basic assumptions of the "New Frontiersmen" should be pondered carefully by those
who look forward to the involvement of academic intellectuals in politics. For example, I have
referred above to Arthur Schlesinger's objections
to the Bay of Pigs invasion, but the reference was
imprecise. True, he felt that it was a "terrible
idea," but "not because the notion of sponsor-
ing an exile attempt to overthrow Castro seemed
intolerable in itself." Such a reaction would be the
merest sentimentality, unthinkable to a tough-
minded realist. The difficulty, rather, was that it
seemed unlikely that the deception could succeed.
The operation, in his view, was ill-conceived but
not otherwise objectionable.[13] In a similar vein,
Schlesinger quotes with approval Kennedy's "realistic" assessment of the situation resulting from
Trujillo's assassination:

*There are three possibilities in descending
order of preference: a decent democratic
regime, a continuation of the Trujillo regime
or a Castro regime. We ought to aim at the
first, but we really can't renounce the second*

*until we are sure that we can avoid the third
[p. 769].*

The reason why the third possibility is so intolerable is explained a few pages later (p. 774): "Communist success in Latin America would deal a much harder blow to the power and influence of the United States." Of course, we can never really be sure of avoiding the third possibility; therefore, in practice, we will always settle for the second, as we are now doing in Brazil and Argentina, for example.[14]

Or consider Walt Rostow's views on American policy in Asia.[15] The basis on which we must build this policy is that "we are openly threatened and we feel menaced by Communist China." To prove that we are menaced is of course unnecessary, and the matter receives no attention; it is enough that we *feel* menaced. Our policy must be based on our national heritage and our national interests. Our national heritage is briefly outlined in the following terms: "Throughout the nineteenth century, in good conscience Americans could devote themselves to the extension of both their principles and their power on this continent," making use of "the somewhat elastic concept of the Monroe doctrine" and, of course, extending "the American interest to Alaska and the mid-Pacific islands. . . . Both our insistence on unconditional surrender and the idea of post-war occupation . . . represented the formulation of American security interests in Europe and Asia." So much for our heritage. As to our interests, the matter is equally simple. Fundamental is our "profound interest that societies abroad develop and strengthen those elements in their respective cultures that elevate and protect the dignity of the individual against the state." At the same time, we must counter the "ideological threat," namely "the possibility that the Chinese Communists can prove to Asians by progress in China that Communist methods are better and faster than democratic methods." Nothing is said about those people in Asian cultures to whom our "conception of the proper relation of the individual to the state" may not be the uniquely important value, people who might, for example, be concerned with preserving the "dignity of the individual" against concentrations of foreign or

To prove that
we are menaced
is of course
unnecessary,
and the matter
receives no attention;
it is enough that
we *feel* menaced.

domestic capital, or against semi-feudal structures (such as Trujillo-type dictatorships) introduced or kept in power by American arms. All of this is flavored with allusions to "our religious and ethical value systems" and to our "diffuse and complex concepts" which are to the Asian mind "so much more difficult to grasp" than Marxist dogma, and are so "disturbing to some Asians" because of "their very lack of dogmatism."

Such intellectual contributions as these suggest the need for a correction to de Gaulle's remark, in his *Memoirs*, about the American "will to power, cloaking itself in idealism." By now, this will to power is not so much cloaked in idealism as it is drowned in fatuity. And academic intellectuals have made their unique contribution to this sorry picture.

+ + + +

LET US, HOWEVER, return to the war in Vietnam and the response that it has aroused among American intellectuals. A striking feature of the recent debate on Southeast Asian policy has been the distinction that is commonly drawn between "responsible criticism," on the one hand, and "sentimental," or "emotional," or "hysterical" criticism, on the other. There is much to be learned from a careful study of the terms in which this distinction is drawn. The "hysterical critics" are to be identified, apparently, by their irrational refusal to accept one fundamental political axiom, namely that the United States has the right to extend its power and control without limit, insofar as is feasible. Responsible criticism does not challenge this assumption, but argues, rather, that we probably can't "get away with it" at this particular time and place.

A distinction of this sort seems to be what Irving Kristol, for example, has in mind in his analysis of the protest over Vietnam policy (*Encounter*, August 1965). He contrasts the responsible critics, such as Walter Lippmann, the *Times*, and Senator Fulbright, with the "teach-in movement." "Unlike the university protesters," he points out, "Mr. Lippmann engages in no presumptuous suppositions as to 'what the Vietnamese people really want'— he obviously doesn't much care—or in legalistic exegesis as to whether, or to what extent, there is

The will to power
is not so much
cloaked in idealism
as it is drowned in
fatuity. And academic
intellectuals have
made their unique
contribution to this
sorry picture.

'aggression' or 'revolution' in South Vietnam. His is a *realpolitik* point of view; and he will apparently even contemplate the possibility of a *nuclear* war against China in extreme circumstances." This is commendable, and contrasts favorably, for Kristol, with the talk of the "unreasonable, ideological types" in the teach-in movement, who often seem to be motivated by such absurdities as "simple, virtuous 'anti-imperialism,'" who deliver "harangues on 'the power structure,'" and who even sometimes stoop so low as to read "articles and reports from the foreign press on the American presence in Vietnam." Furthermore, these nasty types are often psychologists, mathematicians, chemists, or philosophers (just as, incidentally, those most vocal in protest in the Soviet Union are generally physicists, literary intellectuals, and others remote from the exercise of power), rather than people with Washington contacts, who, of course, realize that "had they a new, good idea about Vietnam, they would get a prompt and respectful hearing" in Washington.

I am not interested here in whether Kristol's characterization of protest and dissent is accurate, but rather in the assumptions on which it rests. Is the purity of American motives a matter that is beyond discussion, or that is irrelevant to discussion? Should decisions be left to "experts" with Washington contacts—even if we assume that they command the necessary knowledge and principles to make the "best" decision, will they invariably do so? And, a logically prior question, is "expertise" applicable—that is, is there a body of theory and of relevant information, not in the public domain, that can be applied to the analysis of foreign policy or that demonstrates the correctness of present actions in some way that psychologists, mathematicians, chemists, and philosophers are incapable of comprehending? Although Kristol does not examine these questions directly, his attitude presupposes answers, answers which are wrong in all cases. American aggressiveness, however it may be masked in pious rhetoric, is a dominant force in world affairs and must be analyzed in terms of its causes and motives. There is no body of theory or significant body of relevant information, beyond the comprehension of the layman, which makes policy immune from criticism. To the extent that "expert knowledge" is applied to world affairs, it is surely appropriate—for a person of any integrity, quite necessary—to question its quality and the goals it serves. These facts seem too obvious to require extended discussion.

+   +   +   +

A CORRECTIVE TO KRISTOL'S curious belief in the administration's openness to new thinking about Vietnam is provided by McGeorge Bundy in a recent issue of *Foreign Affairs* (January 1967). As Bundy correctly observes, "on the main stage . . . the argument on Viet Nam turns on tactics, not fundamentals," although, he adds, "there are wild men in the wings." On stage center are, of course, the president (who in his recent trip to Asia had just "magisterially reaffirmed" our interest "in the progress of the people across the Pacific") and his advisers, who deserve "the understanding support of those who want restraint." It is these men who deserve the credit for the fact that "the bombing of the North has been the most accurate

and the most restrained in modern warfare"—
a solicitude which will be appreciated by the
inhabitants, or former inhabitants, of Nam Dinh
and Phu Ly and Vinh. It is these men, too, who
deserve the credit for what was reported by Mal-
colm Browne as long ago as May 1965:

> In the South, huge sectors of the nation
> have been declared "free bombing zones,"
> in which anything that moves is a legitimate
> target. Tens of thousands of tons of bombs,
> rockets, napalm and cannon fire are poured
> into these vast areas each week. If only by the
> laws of chance, bloodshed is believed to be
> heavy in these raids.

Fortunately for the developing countries, Bundy
assures us, "American democracy has no taste for
imperialism," and "taken as a whole, the stock
of American experience, understanding, sympa-
thy and simple knowledge is now much the most
impressive in the world." It is true that "four-fifths
of all the foreign investing in the world is now done

by Americans" and that "the most admired plans and policies . . . are no better than their demonstrable relation to the American interest"—just as it is true, so we read in the same issue of *Foreign Affairs*, that the plans for armed action against Cuba were put into motion a few weeks after Mikoyan visited Havana, "invading what had so long been an almost exclusively American sphere of influence." Unfortunately, such facts as these are often taken by unsophisticated Asian intellectuals as indicating a "taste for imperialism." For example, a number of Indians have expressed their "near exasperation" at the fact that "we have done everything we can to attract foreign capital for fertilizer plants, but the American and the other Western private companies know we are over a barrel, so they demand stringent terms which we just cannot meet" (*Christian Science Monitor*, November 26), while "Washington . . . doggedly insists that deals be made in the private sector with private enterprise" (*ibid.*, December 5).[16] But this reaction, no doubt, simply reveals, once again, how the Asian mind fails to comprehend the "diffuse and complex concepts" of Western thought.

✦ ✦ ✦ ✦

IT MAY BE USEFUL to study carefully the "new, good ideas about Vietnam" that are receiving a "prompt and respectful hearing" in Washington these days. The U.S. Government Printing Office is an endless source of insight into the moral and intellectual level of this expert advice. In its publications one can read, for example, the testimony of Professor David N. Rowe, director of graduate studies in international relations at Yale University, before the House Committee on Foreign Affairs (see note 11). Professor Rowe proposes (p. 266) that the United States buy all surplus Canadian and Australian wheat, so that there will be mass starvation in China. These are his words:

> Mind you, I am not talking about this as a weapon against the Chinese people. It will be. But that is only incidental. The weapon will be a weapon against the Government because the internal stability of that country

cannot be sustained by an unfriendly Government in the face of general starvation.

Professor Rowe will have none of the sentimental moralism that might lead one to compare this suggestion with, say, the *Ostpolitik* of Hitler's Germany.[17] Nor does he fear the impact of such policies on other Asian nations, for example, Japan. He assures us, from his "very long acquaintance with Japanese questions," that "the Japanese above all are people who respect power and determination." Hence "they will not be so much alarmed by American policy in Vietnam that takes off from a position of power and intends to seek a solution based upon the imposition of our power upon local people that we are in opposition to." What would disturb the Japanese is "a policy of indecision, a policy of refusal to face up to the problems [in China and Vietnam] and to meet our responsibilities there in a positive way," such as the way just cited. A conviction that we were "unwilling to use the power that they know we have" might "alarm the Japanese people very intensely and shake the degree of their friendly relations with us." In fact, a full use of American power would be particularly reassuring to the Japanese, because they have had a demonstration "of the tremendous power in action of the United States . . . because they have felt our power directly." This is surely a prime example of the healthy, "*realpolitik* point of view" that Irving Kristol so much admires.

But, one may ask, why restrict ourselves to such indirect means as mass starvation? Why not bombing? No doubt this message is implicit in the remarks to the same committee of the Reverend R.J. de Jaegher, regent of the Institute of Far Eastern Studies, Seton Hall University, who explains that like all people who have lived under Communism, the North Vietnamese "would be perfectly happy to be bombed to be free" (p. 345).

Of course, there must be those who support the Communists. But this is really a matter of small concern, as the Honorable Walter Robertson, assistant secretary of state for Far Eastern affairs from 1953 to 1959, points out in his testimony before the same committee. He assures us that

It may be that
as honest men
the students and
junior faculty are
attempting to find
out the truth for
themselves rather
than ceding the
responsibility to
"experts" or to
government.

"The Peiping regime . . . represents something less than 3 per cent of the population" (p. 402).

Consider, then, how fortunate the Chinese Communist leaders are, compared to the leaders of the Vietcong, who, according to Arthur Goldberg (*New York Times*, February 6, 1966), represent about "one-half of one percent of the population of South Vietnam," that is, about one-half the number of new Southern recruits for the Vietcong during 1965, if we can credit Pentagon statistics.[18]

In the face of such experts as these, the scientists and philosophers of whom Kristol speaks would clearly do well to continue to draw their circles in the sand.

+ + + +

HAVING SETTLED THE ISSUE of the political irrelevance of the protest movement, Kristol turns to the question of what motivates it—more generally, what has made students and junior faculty "go left," as he sees it, amid general prosperity and under liberal, Welfare State administrations. This, he notes, "is a riddle to which no sociologist has as yet come up with an answer." Since these young people are well-off, have good futures, etc., their protest must be irrational. It must be the result of boredom, of too much security, or something of this sort.

Other possibilities come to mind. It may be, for example, that as honest men the students and junior faculty are attempting to find out the truth for themselves rather than ceding the responsibility to "experts" or to government; and it may be that they react with indignation to what they discover. These possibilities Kristol does not reject. They are simply unthinkable, unworthy of consideration. More accurately, these possibilities are inexpressible; the categories in which they are formulated (honesty, indignation) simply do not exist for the tough-minded social scientist.

+ + + +

IN THIS IMPLICIT disparagement of traditional intellectual values, Kristol reflects attitudes that are fairly widespread in academic circles. I do not doubt that these attitudes are in part a consequence of the desperate attempt of the social and behavioral sciences to imitate the surface features of sciences that really have significant intellectual content. But they have other sources as well. Anyone can be a moral individual, concerned with human rights and problems; but only a college professor, a trained expert, can solve technical problems by "sophisticated" methods. Ergo, it is only problems of the latter sort that are important or real. Responsible, nonideological experts will give advice on tactical questions; irresponsible, "ideological types" will "harangue" about principle and trouble themselves over moral issues and human rights, or over the traditional problems of man and society, concerning which "social and behavioral science" has nothing to offer beyond trivialities. Obviously, these emotional, ideological types are irrational, since, being well-off and having power in their grasp, they shouldn't worry about such matters.

At times this pseudoscientific posing reaches levels that are almost pathological. Consider the phenomenon of Herman Kahn, for example. Kahn has been both denounced as immoral and lauded for his courage. By people who should know better, his *On Thermonuclear War* has been described "without qualification . . . [as] . . . one of the great works of our time" (Stuart Hughes). The fact of the matter is that this is surely one of the emptiest works of our time, as can be seen by applying to it the intellectual standards of any existing discipline, by tracing some of its "well-documented conclusions" to the "objective studies" from which they derive, and by following the line of argument, where detectable. Kahn proposes no theories, no explanations, no factual assumptions that can be tested against their consequences, as do the sciences he is attempting to mimic. He simply suggests a terminology and provides a facade of rationality. When particular policy conclusions are drawn, they are supported only by *ex cathedra* remarks for which no support is even suggested (e.g., "The civil defense line probably should be drawn somewhere below $5 billion annually" to keep from provoking the Russians—why not $50 billion, or $5.00?). What is more, Kahn is quite aware of this vacuity; in his more judicious moments he claims only that "there is no reason to believe that relatively sophisticated models are more likely to be misleading than the simpler models and analogies frequently used as an aid to judgment." For those whose humor tends towards the macabre, it is easy to play the game of "strategic thinking" *à la* Kahn, and to prove what one wishes. For example, one of Kahn's basic assumptions is that

> *an all-out surprise attack in which all resources are devoted to counter-value targets would be so irrational that, barring an incredible lack of sophistication or actual insanity among Soviet decision makers, such an attack is highly unlikely.*

A simple argument proves the opposite. *Premise 1:* American decision-makers think along the lines outlined by Herman Kahn. *Premise 2*: Kahn thinks it would be better for everyone to be red than for everyone to be dead. *Premise 3*: if the Americans were to respond to an all-out countervalue attack, then everyone would be dead. *Conclusion*: the Americans will not respond to an all-out countervalue attack, and therefore it should be launched without delay. Of course, one can carry the argument a step further. *Fact*: the Russians have not carried out an all-out counter-value attack. It follows that they are not rational. If they are not rational, there is no point in "strategic thinking." Therefore . . .

Of course this is all nonsense, but nonsense that differs from Kahn's only in the respect that the argument is of slightly greater complexity than anything to be discovered in his work. What is remarkable is that serious people actually pay attention to these absurdities, no doubt because of the facade of tough-mindedness and pseudoscience.

+ + + +

IT IS A CURIOUS and depressing fact that the "anti-war movement" falls prey all too often to similar confusions. In the fall of 1965, for example, there was an International Conference on Alternative Perspectives on Vietnam, which circulated a pamphlet to potential participants stating its assumptions. The plan was to set up study groups in which three "types of intellectual tradition" will be represented: (1) area specialists; (2) "social theory, with special emphasis on theories of the international system, of social change and development, of conflict and conflict resolution, or of revolution"; (3) "the analysis of public policy in terms of basic human values, rooted in various theological, philosophical and humanist traditions." The second intellectual tradition will provide "general propositions, derived from social theory and tested against historical, comparative, or experimental data"; the third "will provide the framework out of which fundamental value questions can be raised and in terms of which the moral implications of societal actions can be analyzed." The hope was that "by approaching the questions [of Vietnam policy] from the moral perspectives of all great religions and philosophical systems, we may find solutions that are more consistent with fundamental human values than current American policy in Vietnam has turned out to be."

In short, the experts on values (i.e., spokesmen for the great religions and philosophical systems) will provide fundamental insights on moral perspectives, and the experts on social theory will provide general empirically validated propositions and "general models of conflict." From this interplay, new policies will emerge, presumably from application of the canons of scientific method. The only debatable issue, it seems to me, is whether it is more ridiculous to turn to experts in social theory for general well-confirmed propositions, or to the specialists in the great religions and philosophical systems for insights into fundamental human values.

There is much more that can be said about this topic but, without continuing, I would simply like to emphasize that, as is no doubt obvious, the cult of the experts is both self-serving, for those who propound it, and fraudulent. Obviously, one must learn from social and behavioral science whatever one can; obviously, these fields should be pursued as seriously as possible. But it will be quite unfortunate, and highly dangerous, if they are not accepted and judged on their merits and according to their actual, not pretended, accomplishments. In particular, if there is a body of theory, well tested and verified, that applies to the conduct

When we consider the responsibility of intellectuals, our basic concern must be their role in the creation and analysis of ideology.

of foreign affairs or the resolution of domestic or international conflict, its existence has been kept a well-guarded secret. In the case of Vietnam, if those who feel themselves to be experts have access to principles or information that would justify what the American government is doing in that unfortunate country, they have been singularly ineffective in making this fact known. To anyone who has any familiarity with the social and behavioral sciences (or the "policy sciences"), the claim that there are certain considerations and principles too deep for the outsider to comprehend is simply an absurdity, unworthy of comment.

✦ ✦ ✦ ✦

WHEN WE CONSIDER THE responsibility of intellectuals, our basic concern must be their role in the creation and analysis of ideology. And, in fact, Kristol's contrast between the unreasonable ideological types and the responsible experts is formulated in terms that immediately bring to mind Daniel Bell's interesting and influential "The End of Ideology," an essay which is as important for what it leaves unsaid as for its actual content.[19]

Bell presents and discusses the Marxist analysis of ideology as a mask for class interest, quoting Marx's well-known description of the belief of the bourgeoisie "that the *special* conditions of its emancipation are the *general* conditions through which alone modern society can be saved and the class struggle avoided." He then argues that the age of ideology is ended, supplanted, at least in the West, by a general agreement that each issue must be settled in its own terms, within the framework of a Welfare State in which, presumably, experts in the conduct of public affairs will have a prominent role. Bell is quite careful, however, to characterize the precise sense of "ideology" in which "ideologies are exhausted." He is referring to ideology only as "the conversion of ideas into social levers," to ideology as "a set of beliefs, infused with passion . . . [which] . . . seeks to transform the whole of a way of life." The crucial words are "transform" and "convert into social levers." Intellectuals in the West, he argues, have lost interest in converting ideas into social levers for the radical transformation of society. Now that we have achieved the pluralistic society of the Welfare State, they see no further need for a radical transformation of society; we may tinker with our way of life here and there, but it would be wrong to try to modify it in any significant way. With this consensus of intellectuals, ideology is dead.

There are several striking facts about Bell's essay. First, he does not point out the extent to which this consensus of the intellectuals is self-serving. He does not relate his observation that, by and large, intellectuals have lost interest in "transforming the whole of a way of life" to the fact that they play an increasingly prominent role in running the Welfare State; he does not relate their general satisfaction with the Welfare State to the fact that, as he observes elsewhere, "America has become an affluent society, offering place . . . and prestige . . . to the onetime radicals." Secondly, he offers no serious argument to show that intellectuals are somehow "right" or "objectively justified" in reaching the consensus to which he alludes, with its rejection of the notion that society should be transformed. Indeed, although Bell is fairly sharp about the empty rhetoric of the "new left," he seems to have a quite utopian faith that technical experts will be able to cope with the few problems that still remain; for example, the fact that labor is treated as a commodity, and the problems of "alienation."

It seems fairly obvious that the classical problems are very much with us; one might plausibly argue that they have even been enhanced in severity and scale. For example, the classical paradox of poverty in the midst of plenty is now an ever-increasing problem on an international scale. Whereas one might conceive, at least in principle, of a solution within national boundaries, a sensible idea of transforming international society to cope with vast and perhaps increasing human misery is hardly likely to develop within the framework of the intellectual consensus that Bell describes.

+ + + +

THUS IT WOULD SEEM natural to describe the consensus of Bell's intellectuals in somewhat different terms from his. Using the terminology of the first part of his essay, we might say that the Welfare State technician finds justification for his special and prominent social status in his "science," specifically, in the claim that social science can support a technology of social tinkering on a domestic or international scale. He then takes a further step, ascribing in a familiar way a universal validity to what is in fact a class interest: he argues that the special conditions on which his claim to power and authority are based are, in fact, the only general conditions by which modern society can be saved; that social tinkering within a Welfare State framework must replace the commitment to the "total ideologies" of the past, ideologies which were concerned with a transformation of society. Having found his position of power, having achieved security and affluence, he has no further need for ideologies that look to radical change. The scholar-expert replaces the "free-floating intellectual" who "felt that the wrong values were being honored, and rejected the society," and who has now lost his political role (now, that is, that the right values are being honored).

Conceivably, it is correct that the technical experts who will (or hope to) manage the "industrial society" will be able to cope with the classical problems without a radical transformation of society. It is conceivably true that the bourgeoisie was right in regarding the special conditions of its emancipation as the only general conditions by which modern society would be saved. In either case, an argument is in order, and skepticism is justified when none appears.

Within the same framework of general utopianism, Bell goes on to pose the issue between Welfare State scholar-experts and third-world ideologists in a rather curious way. He points out, quite correctly, that there is no issue of Communism, the content of that doctrine having been "long forgotten by friends and foes alike." Rather, he says,

> the question is an older one: whether new societies can grow by building democratic institutions and allowing people to make choices—and sacrifices—voluntarily, or whether the new elites, heady with power, will impose totalitarian means to transform their societies.

+ + + +

THE QUESTION IS AN interesting one. It is odd, however, to see it referred to as "an older one." Surely he cannot be suggesting that the West chose the democratic way—for example, that in England during the industrial revolution, the farmers voluntarily made the choice of leaving the land, giving up cottage industry, becoming an industrial proletariat, and voluntarily decided, within the framework of the existing democratic institutions, to make the sacrifices that are graphically described in the classic literature on nineteenth-century industrial society. One may debate the question whether authoritarian control is necessary to permit capital accumulation in the underdeveloped world, but the Western model of development is hardly one that we can point to with any pride. It is perhaps not surprising to find Walt Rostow referring to "the more humane processes [of industrialization] that Western values would suggest" (*An American Policy in Asia*). Those who have a serious concern for the problems that face backward countries, and for the role that advanced industrial societies might, in principle, play in development and modernization, must use somewhat more care in interpreting the significance of the Western experience.

Returning to the quite appropriate question, whether "new societies can grow by building democratic institutions" or only by totalitarian means, I think that honesty requires us to recognize that this question must be directed more to American intellectuals than to third-world ideologists. The backward countries have incredible, perhaps insurmountable problems, and few available options; the United States has a wide range of options, and has the economic and technological resources, though, evidently, neither the intellectual nor moral resources, to confront at least some of these problems. It is easy for an American intellectual to deliver homilies on the virtues of freedom and liberty, but if he is really concerned about, say, Chinese totalitarianism or the burdens imposed on the Chinese peasantry in forced industrialization, then he should face a task that is infinitely more important and challenging—the task of creating, in the United States, the intellectual and moral climate, as well as the social and economic conditions, that would permit this country to participate in

Large gifts to Cuba and China might not succeed in alleviating the authoritarianism, but they are far more likely to help than lectures on democratic values.

modernization and development in a way commensurate with its material wealth and technical capacity. Large capital gifts to Cuba and China might not succeed in alleviating the authoritarianism and terror that tend to accompany early stages of capital accumulation, but they are far more likely to have this effect than lectures on democratic values. It is possible that even without "capitalist encirclement" in its various manifestations, the truly democratic elements in revolutionary movements—in some instances, soviets and collectives—might be undermined by an "elite" of bureaucrats and technical intelligentsia. But it is almost certain that capitalist encirclement itself, which all revolutionary movements now have to face, will guarantee this result. The lesson, for those who are concerned to strengthen the democratic, spontaneous, and popular elements in developing societies, is quite clear. Lectures on the two-party system, or even on the really substantial democratic values that have been in part realized in Western society, are a monstrous irrelevance, given the effort required to raise the level of culture in Western society to the point where it can provide a "social lever" for both economic development and the development of true democratic institutions in the third world—and, for that matter, at home.

+ + + +

A GOOD CASE CAN be made for the conclusion that there is indeed something of a consensus among intellectuals who have already achieved power and affluence, or who sense that they can achieve them by "accepting society" as it is and promoting the values that are "being honored" in this society. It is also true that this consensus is most noticeable among the scholar-experts who are replacing the free-floating intellectuals of the past. In the university, these scholar-experts construct a "value-free technology" for the solution of technical problems that arise in contemporary society,[20] taking a "responsible stance" towards these problems, in the sense noted earlier. This consensus among the responsible scholar-experts is the domestic analogue to that proposed, internationally, by those who justify the application of American power in Asia, whatever the human cost, on the grounds that it is necessary to contain the "expansion of China" (an "expansion" which is, to be sure, hypothetical for the time being)[21]—that is, to translate from State Department Newspeak, on the grounds that it is essential to reverse the Asian nationalist revolutions or, at least, to prevent them from spreading. The analogy becomes clear when we look carefully at the ways in which this proposal is formulated. With his usual lucidity, Churchill outlined the general position in a remark to his colleague of the moment, Joseph Stalin, at Tehran in 1943:

The government of the world must be entrusted to satisfied nations, who wished nothing more for themselves than what they had. If the world-government were in the hands of hungry nations there would always be danger. But none of us had any reason to seek for anything more. . . . Our power placed us above the rest. We were like the rich men dwelling at peace within their habitations.

For a translation of Churchill's biblical rhetoric into the jargon of contemporary social science, one may turn to the testimony of Charles Wolf, senior economist of the Rand Corporation, at the Congressional Committee Hearings cited earlier:

> *I am dubious that China's fears of encirclement are going to be abated, eased, relaxed in the long-term future. But I would hope that what we do in Southeast Asia would help to develop within the Chinese body politic more of a realism and willingness to live with this fear than to indulge it by support for liberation movements, which admittedly depend on a great deal more than external support. . . . The operational question for American foreign policy is not whether that fear can be eliminated or substantially alleviated, but whether China can be faced with a structure of incentives, of penalties and rewards, of inducements that will make it willing to live with this fear.*

The point is further clarified by Thomas Schelling: "There is growing experience, which the Chinese can profit from, that although the

United States may be interested in encircling them, may be interested in defending nearby areas from them, it is, nevertheless, prepared to behave peaceably if they are."

In short, we are prepared to live peaceably in our—to be sure, rather extensive—habitations. And, quite naturally, we are offended by the undignified noises from the servants' quarters. If, let us say, a peasant-based revolutionary movement tries to achieve independence from foreign powers and the domestic structures they support, or if the Chinese irrationally refuse to respond properly to the schedule of reinforcement that we have prepared for them—if they object to being encircled by the benign and peace-loving "rich men" who control the territories on their borders as a natural right—then, evidently, we must respond to this belligerence with appropriate force.

+ + + +

IT IS THIS MENTALITY that explains the frankness with which the U.S. government and its academic apologists defend the American refusal to permit a political settlement in Vietnam at a local level, a settlement based on the actual distribution of political forces. Even government experts freely admit that the NLF is the only "truly mass-based political party in South Vietnam"[22]; that the NLF had "made a conscious and massive effort to extend political participation, even if it was manipulated, on the local level so as to involve the people in a self-contained, self-supporting revolution" (p. 374); and that this effort had been so successful that no political groups, "with the possible exception of the Buddhists, thought themselves equal in size and power to risk entering into a coalition, fearing that if they did the whale would swallow the minnow" (p. 362). Moreover, they concede that until the introduction of overwhelming American force, the NLF had insisted that the struggle "should be fought out at the political level and that the use of massed military might was in itself illegitimate. . . . The battleground was to be the minds and loyalties of the rural Vietnamese, the weapons were to be ideas" (pp. 91–92; cf. also pp. 93, 99–108, 155f.); and, correspondingly, that until mid-1964, aid from Hanoi "was largely confined to two areas—doctrinal know-how and leadership personnel" (p. 321). Captured NLF documents contrast the enemy's "military superiority" with their own "political superiority" (p. 106), thus fully confirming the analysis of American military spokesmen who define our problem as how, "with considerable armed force but little political power, [to] contain an adversary who has enormous political force but only modest military power."[23]

Similarly, the most striking outcome of both the Honolulu conference in February and the Manila conference in October was the frank admission by high officials of the Saigon government that "they could not survive a 'peaceful settlement' that left the Vietcong *political* structure in place even if the Vietcong guerilla units were disbanded," that "they are not able to compete *politically* with the Vietnamese Communists" (Charles Mohr, *New York Times*, February 11, 1966, italics mine). Thus, Mohr continues, the Vietnamese demand a "pacification program" which will have as "its core . . . the destruction of the clandestine Vietcong political structure and the creation of an iron-like system of government political control over the population." And from Manila, the same correspondent, on October 23, quotes a high South Vietnamese official as saying that:

Frankly, we are not strong enough now to compete with the Communists on a purely political basis. They are organized and disciplined. The non-Communist nationalists are not—we do not have any large, well-organized political parties and we do not yet have unity. We cannot leave the Vietcong in existence.

Officials in Washington understand the situation very well. Thus Secretary Rusk has pointed out that "if the Vietcong come to the conference table as full partners they will, in a sense, have been victorious in the very aims that South Vietnam and the United States are pledged to prevent" (January 28, 1966). Max Frankel reported from Washington in the *Times* on February 18, 1966, that

Compromise has had no appeal here because the Administration concluded long

ago that the non-Communist forces of South Vietnam could not long survive in a Saigon coalition with Communists. It is for that reason—and not because of an excessively rigid sense of protocol—that Washington has steadfastly refused to deal with the Vietcong or recognize them as an independent political force.

In short, we will—magnanimously—permit Vietcong representatives to attend negotiations only if they will agree to identify themselves as agents of a foreign power and thus forfeit the right to participate in a coalition government, a right which they have now been demanding for a half-dozen years. We well know that in any representative coalition, our chosen delegates could not last a day without the support of American arms. Therefore, we must increase American force and resist meaningful negotiations, until the day when a client government can exert both military and political control over its own population—a day which may never dawn, for as William Bundy has pointed out, we could never be sure of the security of a Southeast

Asia "from which the Western presence was effectively withdrawn." Thus if we were to "negotiate in the direction of solutions that are put under the label of neutralization," this would amount to capitulation to the Communists.[24] According to this reasoning, then, South Vietnam must remain, permanently, an American military base.

All of this is, of course, reasonable, so long as we accept the fundamental political axiom that the United States, with its traditional concern for the rights of the weak and downtrodden, and with its unique insight into the proper mode of development for backward countries, must have the courage and the persistence to impose its will by force until such time as other nations are prepared to accept these truths—or simply to abandon hope.

+ + + +

IF IT IS THE responsibility of the intellectual to insist upon the truth, it is also his duty to see events in their historical perspective. Thus one must applaud the insistence of the secretary of state on the importance of historical analogies, the Munich analogy, for example. As Munich

If it is the
responsibility of
the intellectual
to insist upon
the truth, it is
also his duty
to see events
in their historical
perspective.

showed, a powerful and aggressive nation with a fanatic belief in its manifest destiny will regard each victory, each extension of its power and authority, as a prelude to the next step. The matter was very well put by Adlai Stevenson, when he spoke of "the old, old route whereby expansive powers push at more and more doors, believing they will open until, at the ultimate door, resistance is unavoidable and major war breaks out." Herein lies the danger of appeasement, as the Chinese tirelessly point out to the Soviet Union—which, they claim, is playing Chamberlain to our Hitler in Vietnam. Of course, the aggressiveness of liberal imperialism is not that of Nazi Germany, though the distinction may seem academic to a Vietnamese peasant who is being gassed or incinerated. We do not want to occupy Asia; we merely wish, to return to Mr. Wolf, "to help the Asian countries progress toward economic modernization, as relatively 'open' and stable societies, to which our access, as a country and as individual citizens, is free and comfortable." The formulation is appropriate. Recent history shows that it makes little difference to us what form of government a country has so long as it remains an "open society," in our peculiar sense of this term—that is, a society that remains open to American economic penetration or political control. If it is necessary to approach genocide in Vietnam to achieve this objective, then this is the price we must pay in defense of freedom and the rights of man.

In pursuing the aim of helping other countries to progress towards open societies, with no thought of territorial aggrandizement, we are breaking no new ground. In the Congressional Hearings that I cited earlier, Hans Morgenthau aptly describes our traditional policy towards China as one which favors "what you might call freedom of competition with regard to the exploitation of China" (*op. cit.*, p. 128). In fact, few imperialist powers have had explicit territorial ambitions. Thus in 1784, the British Parliament announced: "To pursue schemes of conquest and extension of dominion in India are measures repugnant to the wish, honor, and policy of this nation." Shortly after this, the conquest of India was in full swing. A century later, Britain announced its intentions in Egypt under the slogan "intervention, reform, withdrawal." It is obvious which parts of this promise were fulfilled within the next half century. In 1936, on the eve of hostilities in North China, the Japanese stated their Basic Principles of National Policy. These included the use of moderate and peaceful means to extend her strength, to promote social and economic development, to eradicate the menace of Communism, to correct the aggressive policies of the great powers, and to secure her position as the stabilizing power in East Asia. Even in 1937, the Japanese government had "no territorial designs upon China." In short, we follow a well-trodden path.

It is useful to remember, incidentally, that the United States was apparently quite willing, as late as 1939, to negotiate a commercial treaty with Japan and arrive at a *modus vivendi* if Japan would "change her attitude and practice towards our rights and interests in China," as Secretary Hull put it. The bombing of Chungking and the rape of Nanking were unpleasant, it is true, but what was really important was our rights and interests in China, as the responsible, unhysterical men of the day saw quite clearly.

It was the closing of the open door by Japan that led inevitably to the Pacific war, just as it is the closing of the open door by "Communist" China itself that may very well lead to the next, and no doubt last, Pacific war.

+ + + +

QUITE OFTEN, the statements of sincere and devoted technical experts give surprising insight into the intellectual attitudes that lie in the background of the latest savagery. Consider, for example, the following comment by the economist Richard Lindholm, in 1959, expressing his frustration over the failure of economic development in "free Vietnam":

> *The use of American aid is determined by how the Vietnamese use their incomes and their savings. The fact that a large portion of the Vietnamese imports financed with American aid are either consumer goods or raw materials used rather directly to meet consumer demands is an indication that the Vietnamese people desire these goods, for*

they have shown their desire by their willing-
ness to use their piasters to purchase them.[25]

In short, the Vietnamese *people* desire Buicks
and air conditioners, rather than sugar-refining
equipment or road-building machinery, as they
have shown by their behavior in a free market.
And however much we may deplore their free
choice, we must allow the people to have their way.
Of course, there are also those two-legged beasts
of burden that one stumbles on in the countryside,
but as any graduate student of political science can
explain, they are not part of a responsible mod-
ernizing elite, and therefore have only a superficial
biological resemblance to the human race.

In no small measure, it is attitudes like this that
lie behind the butchery in Vietnam, and we had
better face up to them with candor, or we will find
our government leading us towards a "final solution" in Vietnam, and in the many Vietnams that
inevitably lie ahead.

Let me finally return to Dwight Macdonald
and the responsibility of intellectuals. Macdonald
quotes an interview with a death-camp paymaster

who burst into tears when told that the Russians would hang him. "Why should they? What have I done?" he asked. Macdonald concludes: "Only those who are willing to resist authority themselves when it conflicts too intolerably with their personal moral code, only they have the right to condemn the death-camp paymaster." The question "What have I done?" is one that we may well ask ourselves, as we read each day of fresh atrocities in Vietnam—as we create, or mouth, or tolerate the deceptions that will be used to justify the next defense of freedom.

Part II

The Responsibility of Intellectuals, Redux: Using Privilege to Challenge the State

Since we often cannot see what is happening before our eyes, it is perhaps not too surprising that what is at a slight distance removed is utterly invisible. We have just witnessed an instructive example: President Obama's dispatch of seventy-nine commandos into Pakistan on May 1 to carry out what was evidently a planned assassination of the prime suspect in the terrorist atrocities of 9/11, Osama bin Laden. Though the target of the operation, unarmed and with no protection, could easily have been apprehended, he was simply murdered, his body dumped at sea without autopsy. The action was deemed "just and necessary" in the liberal press. There will be no trial, as there was in the case of Nazi criminals—a fact not overlooked by legal authorities abroad who approve of the operation but object to the procedure. As Elaine Scarry reminds us, the prohibition of assassination in international law traces back to a forceful denunciation of the practice by Abraham Lincoln, who condemned the call for assassination as "international outlawry" in 1863, an "outrage," which "civilized nations" view with "horror" and merits the "sternest retaliation."

In 1967, writing about the deceit and distortion surrounding the American invasion of Vietnam, I discussed the responsibility of intellectuals, borrowing the phrase from an important essay of Dwight Macdonald's after World War II. With the tenth anniversary of 9/11 arriving, and widespread approval in the United States of the assassination of the chief suspect, it seems a fitting time to revisit that issue. But before thinking about the responsibility of intellectuals, it is worth clarifying to whom we are referring.

The concept of intellectuals in the modern sense gained prominence with the 1898 "Manifesto of the Intellectuals" produced by the Dreyfusards, who, inspired by Émile Zola's open letter of protest to France's president, condemned both the framing of French artillery officer Alfred

Dreyfus on charges of treason and the subsequent military cover-up. The Dreyfusards' stance conveys the image of intellectuals as defenders of justice, confronting power with courage and integrity. But they were hardly seen that way at the time. A minority of the educated classes, the Dreyfusards were bitterly condemned in the mainstream of intellectual life, in particular by prominent figures among "the immortals of the strongly anti-Dreyfusard Académie Française," Steven Lukes writes. To the novelist, politician, and anti-Dreyfusard leader Maurice Barrès, Dreyfusards were "anarchists of the lecture-platform." To another of these immortals, Ferdinand Brunetière, the very word "intellectual" ignified "one of the most ridiculous eccentricities of our time—I mean the pretension of raising writers, scientists, professors and philologists to the rank of supermen," who dare to "treat our generals as idiots, our social institutions as absurd and our traditions as unhealthy."

Who then were the intellectuals? The minority inspired by Zola (who was sentenced to jail for libel, and fled the country)? Or the immortals of the academy? The question resonates through the ages, in one or another form, and today offers a framework for determining the "responsibility of intellectuals." The phrase is ambiguous: does it refer to intellectuals' moral responsibility as decent human beings in a position to use their privilege and status to advance the causes of freedom, justice, mercy, peace, and other such sentimental concerns? Or does it refer to the role they are expected to play, serving, not derogating, leadership and established institutions?

+ + + +

ONE ANSWER CAME during World War I, when prominent intellectuals on all sides lined up enthusiastically in support of their own states.

In their "Manifesto of 93 German Intellectuals," leading figures in one of the world's most enlightened states called on the West to "have faith in us! Believe, that we shall carry on this war to the end as a civilized nation, to whom the legacy of a Goethe, a Beethoven, and a Kant, is just as sacred as its own hearths and homes." Their counterparts on the other side of the intellectual trenches matched them in enthusiasm for the noble cause, but went beyond in self-adulation. In the *New Republic* they proclaimed, "The effective and decisive work on behalf of the war has been accomplished by . . . a class which must be comprehensively but loosely described as the 'intellectuals.'" These progressives believed they were ensuring that the United States entered the war "under the influence of a moral verdict reached, after the utmost deliberation by the more thoughtful members of the community." They were, in fact, the victims of concoctions of the British Ministry of Information, which secretly sought "to direct the thought of most of the world," but particularly the thought of American progressive intellectuals who might help to whip a pacifist country into war fever.

John Dewey was impressed by the great "psychological and educational lesson" of the war, which proved that human beings—more precisely, "the intelligent men of the community"—can "take hold of human affairs and manage them . . . deliberately and intelligently" to achieve the ends sought, admirable by definition.

Not everyone toed the line so obediently, of course. Notable figures such as Bertrand Russell, Eugene Debs, Rosa Luxemburg, and Karl Liebknecht were, like Zola, sentenced to prison. Debs was punished with particular severity—a ten-year prison term for raising questions about President Wilson's "war for democracy and human rights." Wilson refused him amnesty after the war ended, though Harding finally relented. Some, such as Thorstein Veblen, were chastised but treated less harshly; Veblen was fired from his position in the Food Administration after preparing a report showing that the shortage of farm labor could be overcome by ending Wilson's brutal persecution of labor, specifically the International Workers of the World. Randolph Bourne was dropped by the progressive journals after criticizing the "league of benevolently imperialistic nations" and their exalted endeavors.

The pattern of praise and punishment is a familiar one throughout history: those who line up in the service of the state are typically praised by the general intellectual community, and those who refuse to line up in service of the state are punished.

Since power
tends to prevail,
intellectuals
who serve their
governments are
considered the
responsible ones.

Thus in retrospect Wilson and the progressive intellectuals who offered him their services are greatly honored, but not Debs. Luxemburg and Liebknecht were murdered and have hardly been heroes of the intellectual mainstream. Russell continued to be bitterly condemned until after his death—and in current biographies still is.

In the 1970s prominent scholars distinguished the two categories of intellectuals more explicitly. A 1975 study, *The Crisis of Democracy*, labeled Brunetière's ridiculous eccentrics "value-oriented intellectuals" who pose a "challenge to democratic government which is, potentially at least, as serious as those posed in the past by aristocratic cliques, fascist movements, and communist parties." Among other misdeeds, these dangerous creatures "devote themselves to the derogation of leadership, the challenging of authority," and they challenge the institutions responsible for "the indoctrination of the young." Some even sink to the depths of questioning the nobility of war aims, as Bourne had. This castigation of the miscreants who question authority and the established order was delivered by the scholars of the liberal internationalist Tri-lateral Commission; the Carter administration was largely drawn from their ranks.

Like the *New Republic* progressives during World War I, the authors of *The Crisis of Democracy* extend the concept of the "intellectual" beyond Brunetière's ridiculous eccentrics to include the better sort as well: the "technocratic and policy-oriented intellectuals," responsible and serious thinkers who devote themselves to the constructive work of shaping policy within established institutions and to ensuring that indoctrination of the young proceeds on course.

It took Dewey only a few years to shift from the responsible technocratic and policy-oriented intellectual of World War I to an anarchist of the lecture platform, as he denounced the "un-free press" and questioned "how far genuine intellectual freedom and social responsibility are possible on any large scale under the existing economic regime."

What particularly troubled the Trilateral scholars was the "excess of democracy" during the time of troubles, the 1960s, when normally passive and apathetic parts of the population entered the political arena to advance their concerns: minorities, women, the young, the old, working people . . . in short, the population, sometimes called the "special interests." They are to be distinguished from those whom Adam Smith called the "masters of mankind," who are "the principal architects" of government policy and pursue their "vile maxim": "All for ourselves and nothing for other people." The role of the masters in the political arena is not deplored, or discussed, in the Trilateral volume, presumably because the masters represent "the national interest," like those who applauded themselves for leading the country to war "after the utmost deliberation by the more thoughtful members of the community" had reached its "moral verdict."

To overcome the excessive burden imposed on the state by the special interests, the Trilateralists called for more "moderation in democracy," a return to passivity on the part of the less deserving, perhaps even a return to the happy days when "Truman had been able to govern the country with the cooperation of a relatively small number of Wall Street lawyers and bankers," and democracy therefore flourished.

The Trilateralists could well have claimed to be adhering to the original intent of the Constitution, "intrinsically an aristocratic document designed to check the democratic tendencies of the period" by delivering power to a "better sort" of people and barring "those who were not rich, well born, or prominent from exercising political power," in the accurate words of the historian Gordon Wood. In Madison's defense, however, we should recognize that his mentality was pre-capitalist. In determining that power should be in the hands of "the wealth of the nation," "the more capable set of men," he envisioned those men on the model of the "enlightened Statesmen" and "benevolent philosopher" of the imagined Roman world. They would be "pure and noble," "men of intelligence, patriotism, property, and independent circumstances" "whose wisdom may best discern the true interest of their country, and whose patriotism and love of justice will be least likely to sacrifice it to temporary or partial considerations." So endowed, these men would "refine and enlarge the public views," guarding the public interest against the "mischiefs" of democratic majorities. In a similar vein, the progressive Wilsonian intellectuals might have taken comfort in the discoveries of the behavioral sciences, explained in 1939 by the psychologist and education theorist Edward Thorndike:

> *It is the great good fortune of mankind that there is a substantial correlation between intelligence and morality including good will toward one's fellows. . . . Consequently our superiors in ability are on the average our benefactors, and it is often safer to trust our interests to them than to ourselves.*

A comforting doctrine, though some might feel that Adam Smith had the sharper eye.

+ + + +

SINCE POWER TENDS to prevail, intellectuals who serve their governments are considered responsible, and value-oriented intellectuals are dismissed or denigrated. At home that is.

With regard to enemies, the distinction between the two categories of intellectuals is retained, but with values reversed. In the old Soviet Union, the value-oriented intellectuals were the honored dissidents, while we had only contempt for the apparatchiks and commissars, the technocratic and policy-oriented intellectuals. Similarly in Iran we honor the courageous dissidents and condemn those who defend the clerical establishment. And elsewhere generally.

The honorable term "dissident" is used selectively. It does not, of course, apply, with its favorable connotations, to value-oriented intellectuals at home or to those who combat U.S.-supported tyranny abroad. Take the interesting case of Nelson Mandela, who was removed from the official terrorist list in 2008, and can now travel to the United States without special authorization.

Twenty years earlier, he was the criminal leader of one of the world's "more notorious terrorist groups," according to a Pentagon report. That is why President Reagan had to support the apartheid regime, increasing trade with South Africa in violation of congressional sanctions and

What particularly troubled the Trilateral scholars was the "excess of democracy" in the 1960s.

supporting South Africa's depredations in neighboring countries, which led, according to a UN study, to 1.5 million deaths. That was only one episode in the war on terrorism that Reagan declared to combat "the plague of the modern age," or, as Secretary of State George Shultz had it, "a return to barbarism in the modern age." We may add hundreds of thousands of corpses in Central America and tens of thousands more in the Middle East, among other achievements. Small wonder that the Great Communicator is worshipped by Hoover Institution scholars as a colossus whose "spirit seems to stride the country, watching us like a warm and friendly ghost," recently honored further by a statue that defaces the American embassy in London.

The Latin American case is revealing. Those who called for freedom and justice in Latin America are not admitted to the pantheon of honored dissidents. For example, a week after the fall of the Berlin Wall, six leading Latin American intellectuals, all Jesuit priests, had their heads blown off on the direct orders of the Salvadoran high command. The perpetrators were from an elite battalion armed and trained by Washington that had already left a gruesome trail of blood and terror, and had just returned from renewed training at the John F. Kennedy Special Warfare Center and School at Fort Bragg, North Carolina. The murdered priests are not commemorated as honored dissidents, nor are others like them throughout the hemisphere. Honored dissidents are those who called for freedom in enemy domains in Eastern Europe, who certainly suffered, but not remotely like their counterparts in Latin America.

The distinction is worth examination, and tells us a lot about the two senses of the phrase "responsibility of intellectuals," and about ourselves. It is not seriously in question, as John Coatsworth writes in the recently published Cambridge University *History of the Cold War*, that from 1960 to "the Soviet collapse in 1990, the numbers of political prisoners, torture victims, and executions of nonviolent political dissenters in Latin America vastly exceeded those in the Soviet Union and its East European satellites." Among the executed were many religious martyrs, and there were mass slaughters as well, consistently supported or initiated by Washington.

Why then the distinction? It might be argued that what happened in Eastern Europe is far more momentous than the fate of the South at our hands. It would be interesting to see the argument spelled out. And also to see the argument explaining why we should disregard elementary moral principles, among them that if we are serious about suffering and atrocities, about justice and rights, we will focus our efforts on where we can do the most good—typically, where we share responsibility for what is being done. We have no difficulty demanding that our enemies follow such principles.

Few of us care, or should, what Andrei Sakharov or Shirin Ebadi say about U.S. or Israeli crimes; we admire them for what they say and do about those of their own states, and the conclusion holds far more strongly for those who live in more free and democratic societies, and therefore have far greater opportunities to act effectively. It is of some interest that in the most respected circles, practice is virtually the opposite of what elementary moral values dictate.

But let us conform and keep only to the matter of historical import.

The U.S. wars in Latin America from 1960 to 1990, quite apart from their horrors, have long-term historical significance. To consider just one important aspect, in no small measure they were wars against the Church, undertaken to crush a terrible heresy proclaimed at Vatican II in 1962, which, under the leadership of Pope John XXIII, "ushered in a new era in the history of the Catholic Church," in the words of the distinguished theologian Hans Küng, restoring the teachings of the gospels that had been put to rest in the fourth century when the Emperor Constantine established Christianity as the religion of the Roman Empire, instituting "a revolution" that converted "the persecuted church" to a "persecuting church." The heresy of Vatican II was taken up by Latin American bishops who adopted the "preferential option for the poor." Priests, nuns, and laypersons then brought the radical pacifist message of the gospels to the poor, helping them organize to ameliorate their bitter fate in the domains of U.S. power.

That same year, 1962, President Kennedy made several critical decisions. One was to shift the mission of the militaries of Latin America from "hemispheric defense"—an anachronism from World War II—to "internal security," in effect, war against the domestic population, if they raise their heads. Charles Maechling, who led U.S. counterinsurgency and internal defense planning from 1961 to 1966, describes the unsurprising consequences of the 1962 decision as a shift from toleration "of the rapacity and cruelty of the Latin American military" to "direct complicity" in their crimes to U.S. support for "the methods of Heinrich Himmler's extermination squads." One major initiative was a military coup in Brazil, planned in Washington and implemented shortly after Kennedy's assassination, instituting a murderous and brutal national security state. The plague of repression then spread through the hemisphere, including the 1973 coup installing the Pinochet dictatorship, and later the most vicious of all, the Argentine dictatorship, Reagan's favorite. Central America's turn—not for the first time—came in the 1980s under the leadership of the "warm and friendly ghost" who is now revered for his achievements.

The murder of the Jesuit intellectuals as the Berlin Wall fell was a final blow in defeating the heresy, culminating a decade of horror in El Salvador that opened with the assassination, by much the same hands, of Archbishop Óscar Romero, the "voice for the voiceless." The victors in the war against the Church declare their responsibility with pride. The School of the Americas (since renamed), famous for its training of Latin American killers, announces as one of its "talking points" that the liberation theology that was initiated at Vatican II was "defeated with the assistance of the US army."

Actually, the November 1989 assassinations were *almost* a final blow. More was needed.

A year later Haiti had its first free election, and to the surprise and shock of Washington, which like others had anticipated the easy victory of its own candidate from the privileged elite, the organized public in the slums and hills elected Jean-Bertrand Aristide, a popular priest committed to liberation theology. The United States at once moved to undermine the elected government and, after the military coup that overthrew it a few months later, lent substantial support to the vicious military junta and its elite supporters. Trade was increased in violation of international sanctions and increased further under Clinton, who also authorized the Texaco oil company to supply the murderous rulers, in defiance of his own directives.

I will skip the disgraceful aftermath, amply reviewed elsewhere, except to point out that in 2004, the two traditional torturers of Haiti, France and the United States, joined by Canada, forcefully intervened, kidnapped President Aristide (who had been elected again), and shipped him off to central Africa. He and his party were effectively barred from the farcical 2010–11 elections, the most recent episode in a horrendous history that goes back hundreds of years and is barely known among the perpetrators of the crimes, who prefer tales of dedicated efforts to save the suffering people from their grim fate.

Another fateful Kennedy decision in 1962 was to send a special forces mission to Colombia, led by General William Yarborough, who advised the Colombian security forces to undertake "paramilitary, sabotage and/or terrorist activities against known communist proponents," activities that "should be backed by the United States." The meaning of the phrase "communist proponents" was spelled out by the respected president of the Colombian Permanent Committee for Human Rights, former Minister of Foreign Affairs Alfredo Vázquez Carrizosa, who wrote that the Kennedy administration "took great pains to transform our regular armies into counterinsurgency brigades, accepting the new strategy of the death squads," ushering in

> what is known in Latin America as the National Security Doctrine. . . . [not] defense against an external enemy, but a way to make the military establishment the masters of the game . . . [with] the right to combat the internal enemy, as set forth in the Brazilian doctrine, the Argentine doctrine, the Uruguayan doctrine, and the Colombian doctrine: it is the right to fight and to

If we are serious
about justice,
we will focus our
efforts where
we share
responsibility
for what is
being done.

exterminate social workers, trade unionists, men and women who are not supportive of the establishment, and who are assumed to be communist extremists. And this could mean anyone, including human rights activists such as myself.

In a 1980 study, Lars Schoultz, the leading U.S. academic specialist on human rights in Latin America, found that U.S. aid "has tended to flow disproportionately to Latin American governments which torture their citizens . . . to the hemisphere's relatively egregious violators of fundamental human rights." That included military aid, was independent of need, and continued through the Carter years. Ever since the Reagan administration, it has been superfluous to carry out such a study. In the 1980s one of the most notorious violators was El Salvador, which accordingly became the leading recipient of U.S. military aid, to be replaced by Colombia when it took the lead as the worst violator of human rights in the hemisphere. Vázquez Carrizosa himself was living under heavy guard in his Bogotá residence when I visited him there in 2001 as part of a mission of Amnesty International, which was opening its year-long campaign to protect human rights defenders in Colombia because of the country's horrifying record of attacks against human rights and labor activists, and mostly the usual victims of state terror: the poor and defenseless. Terror and torture in Colombia were supplemented by chemical warfare ("fumigation"), under the pretext of the war on drugs, leading to huge flight to urban slums and misery for the survivors. Colombia's attorney general's office now estimates that more than 140,000 people have been killed by paramilitaries, often acting in close collaboration with the U.S.-funded military.

Signs of the slaughter are everywhere. On a nearly impassable dirt road to a remote village in southern Colombia a year ago, my companions and I passed a small clearing with many simple crosses marking the graves of victims of a paramilitary attack on a local bus. Reports of the killings are graphic enough; spending a little time with the survivors, who are among the kindest and most compassionate people I have ever had the privilege of meeting, makes the picture more vivid, and only more painful.

This is the briefest sketch of terrible crimes for which Americans bear substantial culpability, and that we could easily ameliorate, at the very least.

But it is more gratifying to bask in praise for courageously protesting the abuses of official enemies, a fine activity, but not the priority of a value-oriented intellectual who takes the responsibilities of that stance seriously.

The victims within our domains, unlike those in enemy states, are not merely ignored and quickly forgotten, but are also cynically insulted. One striking illustration came a few weeks after the murder of the Latin American intellectuals in El Salvador. Václav Havel visited Washington and addressed a joint session of Congress. Before his enraptured audience, Havel lauded the "defenders of freedom" in Washington who "understood the responsibility that flowed from" being "the most powerful nation on earth"—crucially, their responsibility for the brutal assassination of his Salvadoran counterparts shortly before.

The liberal intellectual class was enthralled by his presentation. Havel reminds us that "we live in a romantic age," Anthony Lewis gushed. Other prominent liberal commentators reveled in Havel's "idealism, his irony, his humanity," as he "preached a difficult doctrine of individual responsibility" while Congress "obviously ached with respect" for his genius and integrity; and asked why America lacks intellectuals so profound, who "elevate morality over self-interest" in this way, praising us for the tortured and mutilated corpses that litter the countries that we have left in misery. We need not tarry on what the reaction would have been had Father Ellacuría, the most prominent of the murdered Jesuit intellectuals, spoken such words at the Duma after elite forces armed and trained by the Soviet Union assassinated Havel and half a dozen of his associates—a performance that is inconceivable.

The assassination of bin Laden, too, directs our attention to our insulted victims. There is much more to say about the operation—including Washington's willingness to face a serious risk of major war and even leakage of fissile materials to

The first 9/11,
unlike the second,
did not change
the world. It was
"nothing of very
great consequence,"
Kissinger said.

jihadis, as I have discussed elsewhere—but let us keep to the choice of name: Operation Geronimo. The name caused outrage in Mexico and was protested by indigenous groups in the United States, but there seems to have been no further notice of the fact that Obama was identifying bin Laden with the Apache Indian chief. Geronimo led the courageous resistance to invaders who sought to consign his people to the fate of "that hapless race of native Americans, which we are exterminating with such merciless and perfidious cruelty, among the heinous sins of this nation, for which I believe God will one day bring [it] to judgement," in the words of the grand strategist John Quincy Adams, the intellectual architect of manifest destiny, uttered long after his own contributions to these sins. The casual choice of the name is reminiscent of the ease with which we name our murder weapons after victims of our crimes: Apache, Blackhawk, Cheyenne . . . We might react differently if the Luftwaffe were to call its fighter planes "Jew" and "Gypsy."

Denial of these "heinous sins" is sometimes explicit. To mention a few recent cases, two years ago in one of the world's leading left-liberal intellectual journals, the *New York Review of Books*, Russell Baker outlined what he learned from the work of the "heroic historian" Edmund Morgan: namely, that when Columbus and the early explorers arrived they "found a continental vastness sparsely populated by farming and hunting people. . . . In the limitless and unspoiled world stretching from tropical jungle to the frozen north, there may have been scarcely more than a million inhabitants." The calculation is off by many tens of millions, and the "vastness" included advanced civilizations throughout the continent. No reactions appeared, though four months later the editors issued a correction, noting that in North America there may have been as many as 18 million people—and, unmentioned, tens of millions more "from tropical jungle to the frozen north." This was all well known decades ago—including the advanced civilizations and the "merciless and perfidious cruelty" of the "extermination"—but not important enough even for a casual phrase. In the *London Review of Books* a year later, the noted historian Mark Mazower mentioned

American "mistreatment of the Native Americans," again eliciting no comment. Would we accept the word "mistreatment" for comparable crimes committed by enemies?

+ + + +

IF THE RESPONSIBILITY OF intellectuals refers to their moral responsibility as decent human beings in a position to use their privilege and status to advance the cause of freedom, justice, mercy, and peace—and to speak out not simply about the abuses of our enemies but, far more significantly, about the crimes in which we are implicated and can ameliorate or terminate if we choose—how should we think of 9/11?

The notion that 9/11 "changed the world" is widely held, understandably. The events of that day certainly had major consequences, domestic and international. One was to lead President Bush to re-declare Ronald Reagan's war on terrorism—the first one has been effectively "disappeared," to borrow the phrase of our favorite Latin American killers and torturers, presumably because the consequences do not fit well with preferred self-images. Another consequence was the invasion of Afghanistan, then Iraq, and more recently military interventions in several other countries in the region and regular threats of an attack on Iran ("all options are open," in the standard phrase). The costs, in every dimension, have been enormous. That suggests a rather obvious question, not asked for the first time: Was there an alternative?

A number of analysts have observed that bin Laden won major successes in his war against the United States. "He repeatedly asserted that the only way to drive the U.S. from the Muslim world and defeat its satraps was by drawing Americans into a series of small but expensive wars that would ultimately bankrupt them," the journalist Eric Margolis writes.

> The United States, first under George W. Bush and then Barack Obama, rushed right into bin Laden's trap. . . . Grotesquely overblown military outlays and debt addiction . . . may be the most pernicious legacy of the man who thought he could defeat the United States.

A report from the Costs of War project at Brown University's Watson Institute for International Studies estimates that the final bill will be $3.2–$4 trillion. Quite an impressive achievement by bin Laden.

That Washington was intent on rushing into bin Laden's trap was evident at once. Michael Scheuer, the senior CIA analyst responsible for tracking bin Laden from 1996 to 1999, writes, "Bin Laden has been precise in telling America the reasons he is waging war on us." The al Qaeda leader, Scheuer continues, "is out to drastically alter U.S. and Western policies toward the Islamic world."

And, as Scheuer explains, bin Laden largely succeeded: "U.S. forces and policies are completing the radicalization of the Islamic world, something Osama bin Laden has been trying to do with substantial but incomplete success since the early 1990s. As a result, I think it is fair to conclude that the United States of America remains bin Laden's only indispensable ally." And arguably remains so, even after his death.

There is good reason to believe that the jihadi movement could have been split and undermined after the 9/11 attack, which was criticized harshly within the movement. Furthermore, the "crime against humanity," as it was rightly called, could have been approached as a crime, with an international operation to apprehend the likely suspects. That was recognized in the immediate aftermath of the attack, but no such idea was even considered by decision makers in government. It seems no thought was given to the Taliban's tentative offer—how serious an offer, we cannot know—to present the al Qaeda leaders for a judicial proceeding.

At the time, I quoted Robert Fisk's conclusion that the horrendous crime of 9/11 was committed with "wickedness and awesome cruelty"—an accurate judgment. The crimes could have been even worse. Suppose that Flight 93, downed by courageous passengers in Pennsylvania, had bombed the White House, killing the president. Suppose that the perpetrators of the crime planned to, and did, impose a military dictatorship that killed thousands and tortured tens of thousands. Suppose the new dictatorship established, with the support of the criminals, an international terror center that helped impose similar torture-and-terror states elsewhere, and, as icing on the cake, brought in a team of economists—call them "the Kandahar boys"— who quickly drove the economy into one of the worst depressions in its history. That, plainly, would have been a lot worse than 9/11.

As we all should know, this is not a thought experiment. It happened. I am, of course, referring to what in Latin America is often called "the first 9/11": September 11, 1973, when the United States succeeded in its intensive efforts to overthrow the democratic government of Salvador Allende in Chile with a military coup that placed General Pinochet's ghastly regime in office. The dictatorship then installed the Chicago Boys—economists trained at the University of Chicago—to reshape Chile's economy. Consider the economic destruction, the torture and kidnappings, and multiply the numbers killed by twenty-five to yield per capita equivalents, and you will see just how much more devastating the first 9/11 was.

The goal of the overthrow, in the words of the Nixon administration, was to kill the "virus" that might encourage all those "foreigners [who] are out to screw us"—screw us by trying to take over their own resources and more generally to pursue a policy of independent development along lines disliked by Washington. In the background was the conclusion of Nixon's National Security Council that if the United States could not control Latin America, it could not expect "to achieve a successful order elsewhere in the world." Washington's "credibility" would be undermined, as Henry Kissinger put it.

The first 9/11, unlike the second, did not change the world. It was "nothing of very great consequence," Kissinger assured his boss a few days later. And judging by how it figures in conventional history, his words can hardly be faulted, though the survivors may see the matter differently.

These events of little consequence were not limited to the military coup that destroyed Chilean democracy and set in motion the horror story that followed. As already discussed, the first 9/11 was just one act in the drama that began in 1962 when Kennedy shifted the mission of the Latin

Privilege
yields
opportunity,
and opportunity
confers
responsibilities.

American militaries to "internal security." The shattering aftermath is also of little consequence, the familiar pattern when history is guarded by responsible intellectuals.

+ + + +

IT SEEMS TO BE close to a historical universal that conformist intellectuals, the ones who support official aims and ignore or rationalize official crimes, are honored and privileged in their own societies, and the value-oriented punished in one or another way. The pattern goes back to the earliest records. It was the man accused of corrupting the youth of Athens who drank the hemlock, much as Dreyfusards were accused of "corrupting souls, and, in due course, society as a whole," and the value-oriented intellectuals of the 1960s were charged with interference with "indoctrination of the young."

In the Hebrew scriptures there are figures who by contemporary standards are dissident intellectuals, called "prophets" in the English translation. They bitterly angered the establishment with their critical geopolitical analysis, their condemnation of the crimes of the powerful, their calls for justice and concern for the poor and suffering. King Ahab, the most evil of the kings, denounced the Prophet Elijah as a hater of Israel, the first "self-hating Jew," or "anti-American" in the modern counterparts. The prophets were treated harshly, unlike the flatterers at the court, who were later condemned as false prophets. The pattern is understandable. It would be surprising if it were otherwise.

As for the responsibility of intellectuals, there does not seem to me to be much to say beyond some simple truths. Intellectuals are typically privileged—merely an observation about usage of the term. Privilege yields opportunity, and opportunity confers responsibilities. An individual then has choices.

Notes

Preface

1. Edward S. Herman and Noam Chomsky, *Manufacturing Consent* (New York: Pantheon, 1988; updated 2002).

2. For more extensive detail on this affair, see Chomsky, *Necessary Illusions* (Boston: South End Press, 1999; 2nd edition, Toronto: House of Anansi Press, 2013), Appendix I.

3. Charles Kadushin, *The American Intellectual Elite* (New York: Little, Brown, 1974).

4. Jamie Fuller, "How Obama Talked About Iraq, from 2002 to 2014," *Washington Post*, June 19, 2014;

Barack Obama, "My Plan for Iraq," *New York Times*, July 14, 2008.

Part I: The Responsibility of Intellectuals

1. Such a research project has now been undertaken and published as a "Citizens' White Paper": Franz Schurmann, Peter Dale Scott, and Reginald Zelnik, *The Politics of Escalation in Vietnam* (New York: Fawcett World Library and Beacon Press, 1966). For further evidence of American rejection of UN initiatives for diplomatic settlement, just prior to the major escalation of February 1965, see Mario Rossi, "The US Rebuff to U Thant: The Untold Story," *New York Review of Books*, November 17, 1966. There is further documentary evidence of NLF attempts to establish a coalition government and to neutralize the area, all rejected by the United States and its Saigon ally, in Douglas Pike, *Viet Cong: The Organization and Techniques of the National Liberation Front of South Vietnam* (Cambridge, MA: M.I.T. Press, 1966). In reading material of this latter sort one must be especially careful to distinguish between the evidence

presented and the "conclusions" that are asserted, for reasons noted briefly below (see note 22).

It is interesting to see the first, somewhat oblique, published reactions to *The Politics of Escalation*, by those who defend our right to conquer South Vietnam and institute a government of our choice. For example, Robert Scalapino (*New York Times Magazine*, December 11, 1966) argues that the thesis of the book implies that our leaders are "diabolical." Since no right-thinking person can believe this, the thesis is refuted. To assume otherwise would betray "irresponsibility," in a unique sense of this term—a sense that gives an ironic twist to the title of this essay. He goes on to point out the alleged central weakness in the argument of the book, namely, the failure to perceive that a serious attempt on our part to pursue the possibilities for a diplomatic settlement would have been interpreted by our adversaries as a sign of weakness.

2. At other times, Schlesinger does indeed display admirable scholarly caution. For example, in his introduction to *The Politics of Escalation* he admits that there may have been "flickers of interest in negotiations" on the part of Hanoi. As to the administration's

lies about negotiations and its repeated actions undercutting tentative initiatives towards negotiations, he comments only that the authors may have underestimated military necessity and that future historians may prove them wrong. This caution and detachment must be compared with Schlesinger's attitude towards renewed study of the origins of the Cold War: in a letter to the *New York Review of Books*, October 20, 1966, he remarks that it is time to "blow the whistle" on revisionist attempts to show that the Cold War may have been the consequence of something more than mere Communist belligerence. We are to believe, then, that the relatively straightforward matter of the origins of the Cold War is settled beyond discussion, whereas the much more complex issue of why the United States shies away from a negotiated settlement in Vietnam must be left to future historians to ponder.

It is useful to bear in mind that the U.S. government itself is on occasion much less diffident in explaining why it refuses to contemplate a meaningful negotiated settlement. As is freely admitted, this solution would leave it without power to control the situation.

3. Arthur M. Schlesinger, Jr., *A Thousand Days: John F. Kennedy in the White House* (Boston and New York: Houghton Mifflin Company, 1965), p. 421.

4. *View from the Seventh Floor* (New York: Harper and Row, 1964), p. 149. See also his *The United States in the World Arena: An Essay in Recent History* (New York: Harper and Row, 1960), p. 244: "Stalin, exploiting the disruption and weakness of the post-war world, pressed out from the expanded base he had won during the second World War in an effort to gain the balance of power in Eurasia . . . turning to the East, to back Mao and to enflame the North Korean and Indochinese Communists."

5. For example, the article by CIA analyst George Carver placed in *Foreign Affairs*, April 1966. See also note 22.

6. Cf. Jean Lacouture, *Vietnam: Between Two Truces* (New York: Random House, 1966), p. 21. Diem's analysis of the situation was shared by Western observers at the time. See, for example, the comments of William Henderson, Far Eastern specialist

and executive, Council on Foreign Relations, in R. W. Lindholm, ed., *Vietnam: The First Five Years* (East Lansing: Michigan State, 1959). He notes "the growing alienation of the intelligentsia," "the renewal of armed dissidence in the South," the fact that "security has noticeably deteriorated in the last two years," all as a result of Diem's "grim dictatorship," and predicts "a steady worsening of the political climate in free Vietnam, culminating in unforeseen disasters."

7. See Bernard Fall, "Vietnam in the Balance," *Foreign Affairs*, October 1966.

8. Stalin was pleased neither by the Titoist tendencies inside the Greek Communist Party, nor by the possibility that a Balkan federation might develop under Titoist leadership. It is, nevertheless, conceivable that Stalin supported the Greek guerrillas at some stage of the rebellion, in spite of the difficulty of obtaining firm documentary evidence. Needless to say, no elaborate study is necessary to document the British or American role in this civil conflict, from late 1944. See Dimitrios G. Kousoulas, *The Price of Freedom: Greece in World Affairs, 1939–1953*

(Syracuse: Syracuse University Press, 1953); *Revolution and Defeat: The Story of the Greek Communist Party* (London and New York: Oxford University Press, 1965), for serious study of these events from a strongly anti-Communist point of view.

9. For a detailed account, see James Warburg, *Germany: Key to Peace* (Cambridge, MA: Harvard University Press, 1953), p. 189f. Warburg concludes that apparently "the Kremlin was now prepared to accept the creation of an All-German democracy in the Western sense of that word," whereas the Western powers, in their response, "frankly admitted their plan 'to secure the participation of Germany in a purely defensive European community'" (i.e., NATO).

10. *United States and the World Arena*, pp. 344–45. Incidentally, those who quite rightly deplore the brutal suppression of the East German and Hungarian revolutions would do well to remember that these scandalous events might have been avoided had the United States been willing to consider proposals for neutralization of Central Europe. Some of George Kennan's recent statements provide interesting commentary on

this matter, for example, his comments on the falsity, from the outset, of the assumption that the USSR intended to attack or intimidate by force the Western half of the continent and that it was deterred by American force, and his remarks on the sterility and general absurdity of the demand for unilateral Soviet withdrawal from Eastern Germany together with "the inclusion of a united Germany as a major component in a Western defense system based primarily on nuclear weaponry" (Edward Reed, ed., *Pacem in Terris: An International Convocation on the Requirements of Peace* [New York: Pocket Books, 1965]).

It is worth noting that historical fantasy of the sort illustrated in Rostow's remarks has become a regular State Department specialty. Thus we have Thomas Mann justifying our Dominican intervention as a response to actions of the "Sino-Soviet military bloc." Or, to take a more considered statement, we have William Bundy's analysis of stages of development of Communist ideology in his Pomona College address, February 12, 1966, in which he characterizes the Soviet Union in the 1920s and early 1930s as "in a highly militant and aggressive phase." What is frightening about fantasy, as distinct from outright falsification, is the possibility that it may be sincere and may actually serve as the basis for formation of policy.

11. *United States Policy Toward Asia*, Hearings before the subcommittee on the Far East and the Pacific of the Committee on Foreign Affairs, House of Representatives, U.S. Government Printing Office, 1966.

12. *New York Times Book Review*, November 20, 1966. Such comments call to mind the remarkable spectacle of President Kennedy counseling Cheddi Jagan on the dangers of entering into a trading relationship "which brought a country into a condition of economic dependence." The reference, of course, is to the dangers in commercial relations with the Soviet Union. See *A Thousand Days*, p. 776.

13. *A Thousand Days*, p. 252.

14. Though this too is imprecise. One must recall the real character of the Trujillo regime to appreciate the full cynicism of Kennedy's "realistic" analysis.

15. W. W. Rostow and R. W. Hatch, *An American Policy in Asia* (Cambridge, MA, and New York: Technology Press and John Wiley, 1955).

16. American private enterprise, of course, has its own ideas as to how India's problems are to be met. The *Monitor* reports the insistence of American entrepreneurs "on importing all equipment and machinery when India has a tested capacity to meet some of their requirements. They have insisted on importing liquid ammonia, a basic raw material, rather than using indigenous naptha which is abundantly available. They have laid down restrictions about pricing, distribution, profits, and management control."

A major postwar scandal is developing in India, as the United States, cynically capitalizing on India's current torture, applies its economic power to implement what the *New York Times* calls India's "drift from socialism towards pragmatism" (April 28, 1965).

17. Although, to maintain perspective, we should recall that in his wildest moments, Alfred Rosenberg spoke of the elimination of thirty million Slavs, not

the imposition of mass starvation on a quarter of the human race. Incidentally, the analogy drawn here is highly "irresponsible," in the technical sense of this neologism discussed earlier. That is, it is based on the assumption that statements and actions of Americans are subject to the same standards and open to the same interpretations as those of anyone else.

18. *New York Times*, February 6, 1966. Goldberg continues, the United States is not certain that all of these are voluntary adherents. This is not the first such demonstration of Communist duplicity. Another example was seen in the year 1962, when according to U.S. government sources 15,000 guerrillas suffered 30,000 casualties. See *A Thousand Days*, p. 982.

19. Reprinted in a collection of essays, *The End of Ideology: On the Exhaustion of Political Ideas in the Fifties* (Glencoe, IL: Free Press, 1960). I have no intention here of entering into the full range of issues that have been raised in the discussion of "end of ideology" for the past dozen years. It is difficult to see how a rational person could quarrel with many of the theses that have been put forth, e.g., that at a certain

historical moment the "politics of civility" is appropriate and, perhaps, efficacious; that one who advocates action (or inaction) has a responsibility to assess its social cost; that dogmatic fanaticism and "secular religions" should be combated (or, if possible, ignored); that technical solutions to problems should be implemented, where possible; that "*le dogmatisme idéologique devait disparaître pour que les idées reprissent vie*" (Aron), and so on. Since this is sometimes taken to be an expression of an "anti-Marxist" position, it is worth keeping in mind that such sentiments as these have no bearing on non-Bolshevik Marxism, as represented, for example, by such figures as Luxemburg, Pannekoek, Korsch, Arthur Rosenberg, and others.

20. The extent to which this "technology" is value-free is hardly very important, given the clear commitments of those who apply it. The problems with which research is concerned are those posed by the Pentagon or the great corporations, not, say, by the revolutionaries of northeast Brazil or by SNCC. Nor am I aware of a research project devoted to the problem of how poorly armed guerrillas might more effectively resist

a brutal and devastating military technology—surely the kind of problem that would have interested the free-floating intellectual who is now hopelessly out of date.

21. In view of the unremitting propaganda barrage on "Chinese expansion," perhaps a word of comment is in order. Typical of American propaganda on this subject is Adlai Stevenson's assessment shortly before his death (cf. the *New York Times Magazine*, March 13, 1966): "So far, the new Communist 'dynasty' has been very aggressive. Tibet was swallowed, India attacked, the Malays had to fight 12 years to resist a 'national liberation' they could receive from the British by a more peaceful route. Today, the apparatus of infiltration and aggression is already at work in North Thailand."

As to Malaya, Stevenson is probably confusing ethnic Chinese with the government of China. Those concerned with the actual events would agree with Harry Miller (in *The Communist Menace in Malaya* [New York: Praeger, 1954]) that "Communist China continues to show little interest in the Malayan affair beyond its usual fulminations via Peking Radio."

There are various harsh things that one might say about Chinese behavior in what the Sino-Indian Treaty of 1954 refers to as "the Tibet region of China," but it is no more proof of a tendency towards expansionism than is the behavior of the Indian government with regard to the Naga and Mizo tribesmen. As to north Thailand, "the apparatus of infiltration" may well be at work, though there is little reason to suppose it to be Chinese—and it is surely not unrelated to the American use of Thailand as a base of its attack on Vietnam. This reference is the sheerest hypocrisy.

The "attack on India" grew out of a border dispute that began several years after the Chinese had completed a road from Tibet to Sinkiang in an area so remote from Indian control that the Indians learned about this operation only from the Chinese press. According to American Air Force maps, the disputed area is in Chinese territory. Cf. Alastair Lamb, *China Quarterly*, July–September, 1965. To this distinguished authority, "it seems unlikely that the Chinese have been working out some master plan . . . to take over the Indian sub-continent lock, stock and overpopulated barrel." Rather, he thinks it likely that the Chinese were probably unaware that India even claimed the territory through which the road passed. After the Chinese military victory, Chinese troops were, in most areas, withdrawn beyond the McMahon line, a border which the British had attempted to impose on China in 1914 but which has never been recognized by China (Nationalist or Communist), the United States, or any other government. It is remarkable that a person in a responsible position could describe all of this as Chinese expansionism. In fact, it is absurd to debate the hypothetical aggressiveness of a China surrounded by American missiles and a still expanding network of military bases backed by an enormous American expeditionary force in Southeast Asia. It is conceivable that at some future time a powerful China may be expansionist. We may speculate about such possibilities if we wish, but it is American aggressiveness that is the central fact of current politics.

22. Douglas Pike, *op. cit.*, p. 110. This book, written by a foreign service officer working at the Center for International Studies, M.I.T., poses a contrast between our side, which sympathizes with "the usual revolutionary stirrings . . . around the world because they reflect inadequate living standards or oppressive

and corrupt governments," and the backers of "revolutionary guerrilla warfare," which "opposes the aspirations of people while apparently furthering them, manipulates the individual by persuading him to manipulate himself." Revolutionary guerrilla warfare is "an imported product, revolution from the outside" (other examples, besides the Vietcong, are "Stalin's exportation of armed revolution," the Haganah in Palestine, and the Irish Republican Army—see pp. 32–33). The Vietcong could not be an indigenous movement since it had "a social construction program of such scope and ambition that of necessity it must have been created in Hanoi" (p. 76—but on pp. 77–79 we read that "organizational activity had gone on intensively and systematically for several years" before the Lao Dong party in Hanoi had made its decision "to begin building an organization"). On page 80 we find "such an effort had to be the child of the North," even though elsewhere we read of the prominent role of the Cao Dai (p. 74), "the first major social group to begin actively opposing the Diem government" (p. 222), and of the Hoa Hao sect, "another early and major participant in the NLF" (p. 69). He takes it as proof of Communist duplicity that in the South, the party insisted it was "Marxist-Leninist," thus "indicating philosophic but not political allegiance," whereas in the North it described itself as a "Marxist-Leninist organization," thus "indicating that it was in the mainstream of the world-wide Communist movement" (p. 150). And so on. Also revealing is the contempt for "Cinderella and all the other fools [who] could still believe there was magic in the mature world if one mumbled the secret incantation: solidarity, union, concord"; for the "gullible, misled people" who were "turning the countryside into a bedlam toppling one Saigon government after another, confounding the Americans"; for the "mighty force of people" who in their mindless innocence thought that "the meek, at last, were to inherit the earth," that "riches would be theirs and all in the name of justice and virtue." One can appreciate the chagrin with which a sophisticated Western political scientist must view this "sad and awesome spectacle."

23. Lacouture, *op. cit.*, p. 188. The same military spokesman goes on, ominously, to say that this is the problem confronting us throughout Asia, Africa, and Latin America, and that we must find the "proper response" to it.

24. William Bundy, in Alastair Buchan, ed., *China and the Peace of Asia* (New York: Praeger, 1965).

25. Lindholm, *op, cit.*

Acknowledgments

"The Responsibility of Intellectuals" originally appeared in the *New York Review of Books*, February 23, 1967, © 1967 by Noam Chomsky.

"The Responsibility of Intellectuals, Redux" originally appeared in the *Boston Review*, September 1, 2011, and is from the book *Who Rules the World?* by Noam Chomsky © 2016 by L. Valeria Galvao-Wasserman-Chomsky. Used by arrangement with Metropolitan Books/Henry Holt and Company. All rights reserved.

About the Author

Noam Chomsky is Institute Professor (emeritus) in the Department of Linguistics and Philosophy at the Massachusetts Institute of Technology and Laureate Professor of Linguistics and Agnese Nelms Haury Chair in the Program in Environment and Social Justice at the University of Arizona. Widely credited with having revolutionized the field of modern linguistics, he is also a political dissident who has written more than one hundred books. His New Press books include *Understanding Power*, *On Anarchism*, and *The Essential Chomsky*. He lives in Cambridge, Massachusetts.

Celebrating 25 Years of Independent Publishing

Thank you for reading this book published by The New Press. The New Press is a nonprofit, public interest publisher celebrating its twenty-fifth anniversary in 2017. New Press books and authors play a crucial role in sparking conversations about the key political and social issues of our day.

We hope you enjoyed this book and that you will stay in touch with The New Press. Here are a few ways to stay up to date with our books, events, and the issues we cover:

* Sign up at www.thenewpress.com/subscribe to receive updates on New Press authors and issues and to be notified about local events

* Like us on Facebook: www.facebook.com/newpressbooks

* Follow us on Twitter: www.twitter.com/thenewpress

Please consider buying New Press books for yourself; for friends and family; and to donate to schools, libraries, community centers, prison libraries, and other organizations involved with the issues our authors write about.

The New Press is a 501(c)(3) nonprofit organization. You can also support our work with a tax-deductible gift by visiting www.thenewpress.com/donate.